THE COMPLETE

DIABETIC

Cookbook for Beginners

1800 Days of Super Easy, Delicious, Low-Sugar & Low-Carbs Recipes with a 30-Day Meal Plan for Type 2 Diabetes and Prediabetes Newly Diagnosed.

Savoring Healthy Living Without Compromising Taste

Julianna Wiggins

TABLE OF CONTENTS

INTRODUCTION

Dear readers,

In the hustle and bustle of our daily lives, health often takes a backseat, and for millions grappling with diabetes and prediabetes, this negligence can have severe consequences. Picture this: a person diagnosed with diabetes, overwhelmed by an avalanche of dietary restrictions and culinary monotony, desperately seeking a way to savor life's flavors once more. Perhaps it's you, or maybe someone you love. The frustration, confusion, and a longing for a taste of normalcy prevail.

Understanding these challenges intimately, we embarked on a culinary odyssey that led to the creation of "The Complete Diabetic Cookbook for Beginners." This book is not just a collection of recipes; it is a beacon of hope for anyone facing the daunting prospect of managing diabetes. Here, within the pages that follow, lies a treasure trove of solutions to the problems that plague your kitchen, your taste buds, and your health.

Imagine a world where diabetes isn't synonymous with deprivation, where meals are not just sustenance but celebrations of life, and where every bite nurtures your body without compromising on taste. That world is not a distant dream but a reality waiting to unfold within these chapters.

Understanding Your Challenges: A Culinary Compass

We comprehend the challenges you face because we have stood where you stand now. The overwhelming array of restrictions, the struggle to plan balanced meals, the fear of losing beloved tastes – we get it. We've witnessed the confusion that comes with deciphering labels, the frustration of unpalatable meals, and the concern for family members' well-being. It was this understanding that fueled our journey to unravel the mysteries of diabetic-friendly cuisine.

Solutions Within Reach: Your Culinary Guidebook

"The Complete Diabetic Cookbook for Beginners" isn't just a cookbook; it's a lifeline. Within these pages, you will discover not just recipes, but a roadmap to flavorful living with diabetes. Each dish has been meticulously crafted to be low in sugar and carbs while abundant in taste. Say goodbye to bland meals and embrace a vibrant palette of flavors designed to tantalize your taste buds.

This book isn't merely about recipes; it's about empowering you to take charge of your health through the joy of cooking. It's about infusing every meal with passion and purpose, transforming your kitchen into a sanctuary of health and happiness.

Your Journey Towards Transformation

Envision a life where diabetes doesn't limit your choices, but expands your culinary horizons.

Picture relishing breakfasts that energize your mornings, indulging in dinners that nourish your body, and savoring desserts that satisfy your sweet cravings without the guilt. With our guidance, you'll embark on a transformative journey, where each recipe is a step toward a healthier, more vibrant you.

Guided by Expertise: Your Trustworthy Companion

Allow us to be your culinary companions on this journey. With years of expertise in both nutrition and the art of cooking, we've curated this book not just as authors but as partners in your health. Our mission is simple – to demystify diabetes, making the path to healthier living not just accessible but delightful.

Through our collective knowledge, we offer you more than just recipes; we provide understanding, compassion, and a genuine desire to see you thrive.

Are you ready to embark on this culinary adventure? Let's begin. Welcome to "The Complete Diabetic Cookbook for Beginners." Your journey to a healthier, tastier life starts now.

Simply scan the QR code provided below to unlock a treasure of exclusive bonuses

CHAPTER 1: UNDERSTANDING THE BASICS OF DIABETES AND DIET

Welcome to our first chapter, where we will delve into the fundamentals of diabetes and diet, providing essential knowledge to help you make informed decisions about your health and well being.

Types of Diabetes: Exploring the Differences

Type 1 diabetes typically develops at an early age and is associated with the inability of the pancreas to produce sufficient insulin. This leads to the body's inability to efficiently use glucose as an energy source. Consequently, individuals with Type 1 diabetes need to receive insulin from external sources to maintain normal blood sugar levels.

Type 2 diabetes, on the other hand, is often linked to lifestyle factors, including diet, physical activity, and stress levels. The pancreas produces insulin, but the body does not respond to it properly, resulting in elevated blood sugar levels. Often, this type of diabetes can be managed with lifestyle changes, including diet and physical activity.

Lastly, prediabetes is a condition where blood sugar levels are higher than normal but not high enough for a diagnosis of Type 2 diabetes. However, prediabetes can serve as a warning sign of potential Type 2 diabetes development in the future.

Why We Are Diagnosed with Diabetes: Unraveling the Causes

Understanding why we are diagnosed with diabetes is crucial in making the necessary changes to lead a healthier life.

Genetic Factors and Lifestyle Choices:

Diabetes, particularly Type 2 diabetes, can have roots in our genes. Some individuals are genetically predisposed to this condition, making them more susceptible. However, genetics is just one piece of the puzzle. Our lifestyle choices play a significant role in the development of diabetes.

Impact of Obesity and Sedentary Habits:

One of the leading causes of Type 2 diabetes is obesity. When our bodies accumulate excess fat, especially around the abdomen, it leads to insulin resistance, where the cells fail to respond to insulin effectively. This resistance results in elevated blood sugar levels, eventually causing diabetes.

Similarly, a sedentary lifestyle contributes significantly to diabetes. Lack of physical activity leads to weight gain and muscle loss, making it harder for the body to regulate blood sugar levels. Regular exercise not only helps in weight management but also improves insulin sensitivity, reducing the risk of diabetes.

Importance of Regular Exercise and Physical Activity:

Physical activity is a cornerstone in the prevention of Type 2 diabetes. Engaging in regular exercise offers multifaceted benefits. Firstly, it aids in weight management by burning excess calories and promoting the development of lean muscle mass. Maintaining a healthy weight is pivotal in reducing the risk of diabetes, as it enhances insulin sensitivity, allowing the body to use insulin more effectively.

Secondly, exercise directly improves insulin sensitivity. When you engage in physical activities like aerobic exercises, your cells become more responsive to insulin, enabling better regulation of blood sugar levels. This effect is particularly beneficial for individuals with insulin resistance, a common precursor to Type 2 diabetes.

Lastly, regular physical activity supports overall cardiovascular health. Diabetes often leads to complications related to the heart and blood vessels. By exercising regularly, you strengthen your heart, improve blood circulation, and reduce the risk of heart diseases associated with diabetes.

Role of Balanced Diet in Prevention:

Equally vital is the role of a balanced diet in diabetes prevention. A diet rich in whole grains, fruits, vegetables, lean proteins, and healthy fats provides essential nutrients without causing drastic spikes in blood sugar levels. Incorporating fiber-rich foods aids in digestion, helps maintain a healthy weight, and stabilizes blood sugar levels.

Avoiding processed foods, sugary beverages, and excessive consumption of refined carbohydrates is key. These foods not only contribute to weight gain but also lead to rapid blood sugar fluctuations, stressing the body's insulin response.

What to Eat and Not to Eat: Crafting a Diabetes-Friendly Diet

Low-Glycemic Index Foods: The Foundation of Healthy Eating

The Glycemic Index (GI) is a crucial tool in diabetes management. It measures how quickly carbohydrate-containing foods raise blood sugar levels. Foods with a low GI are digested and absorbed more slowly, causing a slower and lower rise in blood sugar levels. These foods are the foundation of a diabetes-friendly diet.

Focus on incorporating whole grains like quinoa, barley, and whole wheat, as well as non starchy vegetables such as leafy greens, broccoli, and cauliflower. Legumes like lentils and chickpeas are excellent choices too, as they are high in fiber and protein, making them ideal for stabilizing blood sugar levels.

Avoiding High Sugar and High Carb Traps

High-sugar and high-carb foods can wreak havoc on blood sugar levels, leading to spikes and crashes that are particularly detrimental for individuals with diabetes. Steer clear of sugary beverages, processed snacks, and desserts laden with refined sugars. Opt for natural sweeteners like stevia or monk fruit when you crave something sweet.

Additionally, limit your intake of refined carbohydrates, including white bread, sugary cereals, and sugary baked goods. These foods are rapidly broken down into sugar in the body, causing sudden spikes in blood glucose levels.

.

Essential Nutritional Information: Understanding Labels and Ingredients

Decoding Food Labels: Hidden Sugars and Carbs

Understanding food labels is a crucial skill for anyone managing diabetes. Often, sugars and carbohydrates are disguised under various names, making it challenging to identify their presence in packaged foods. Keep an eye out for terms like sucrose, fructose, and corn syrup, which all indicate added sugars. Likewise, be cautious about ingredients ending in "-ose," as they are likely forms of sugar.

Carbohydrates can also be tricky to spot, especially in processed foods. Ingredients like white flour, rice, and cornstarch are high in carbs and can cause rapid spikes in blood sugar levels. Opt for products with whole grains and natural sweeteners, as they generally have a lower glycemic index and are better for managing blood glucose.

Ingredients to Avoid for Diabetics

Sugar and Its Derivatives:

- Sucrose
- Fructose
- Glucose
- Corn Syrup
- Honey
- Maltodextrin

Carbohydrates and Carbohydrate Products:

- White Flour
- Potato Starch
- Rice
- Bread
- Dough
- Potatoes

Trans Fats and Saturated Fats:

- Hydrogenated Oils
- Trans Fats
- Palm Oil

Salt:

Excessive salt consumption can raise blood pressure and negatively impact heart health.

Natural Flavors and Additives:

Artificial and natural flavors may contain hidden sugars and carbohydrates.

Preservatives:

Some preservatives can affect blood glucose levels.

Artificial Sweeteners:

- Aspartame
- Sucralose
- Saccharin
- Acesulfame Potassium

This list serves as a general guide and may vary based on specific needs and doctor's recommendations. It's always crucial to read product labels carefully and avoid items high in sugar, carbohydrates, and trans fats.

Identifying Nutrient-Rich Foods for Optimal Health

In your quest for balanced nutrition, focus on nutrient-dense foods that provide essential vitamins, minerals, and fiber without significantly impacting blood sugar levels. Incorporate a variety of colorful vegetables, such as leafy greens, bell peppers, and carrots, into your meals. These vegetables are rich in vitamins and antioxidants while being relatively low in calories and carbs.

Additionally, choose lean sources of protein like poultry, fish, tofu, and legumes. Protein not only aids in muscle repair and growth but also helps maintain stable blood sugar levels when consumed alongside carbohydrates.

Ingredients Suitable for Diabetics

Healthy Proteins:

- Chicken
- Turkey
- Fish
- Eggs
- Tofu
- Almond Butter

Low-Fat Dairy:

- Skim Milk
- Low-Fat Yogurt
- Low-Fat Cottage Cheese

Low-Carb Carbohydrates:

- Quinoa
- Brown Rice
- Vegetables
- Low-Sugar Fruits (such as berries and citrus fruits)

Healthy Fats:

- Olive Oil
- Avocado
- Nuts

Natural Sweeteners:

- Stevia
- Erythritol
- Honey in moderation

Dietary Fiber:

- Whole Grains
- Vegetables
- Fruits

Low-Sugar Products:

- Raw Nuts and Seeds
- Unsweetened Dairy Products
- Unsweetened Natural Juices

This list can help you choose nutrient-rich foods suitable for managing blood glucose levels. It is always recommended to consult with a doctor or nutritionist to develop an individualized meal plan.

Practical Tips for Diabetes-Friendly Cooking: Making Every Meal Count

When it comes to managing diabetes, your approach to cooking is just as important as the ingredients you choose. Here are some practical tips to ensure every meal is diabetes-friendly, nutritious, and delicious:

Cooking Techniques to Preserve Nutrients

Steam, Don't Boil: Steaming vegetables preserves their nutrients while enhancing their natural flavors. Avoid boiling, which can leach essential vitamins into the water.

Roasting and Grilling: Roasting vegetables and lean meats at moderate temperatures can bring out their sweetness without adding extra fats. Grilling achieves a similar effect and adds a smoky flavor.

Stir-Frying: Stir-frying with a small amount of heart-healthy oil at high heat cooks ingredients quickly, retaining their nutrients and natural colors.

Slow Cooking: Using a slow cooker allows flavors to meld while keeping nutrients intact. It's an excellent method for soups, stews, and legumes.

Microwaving: Believe it or not, microwaving can preserve nutrients due to its short cooking time. Use microwave-safe containers and a small amount of water to steam vegetables.

Smart Substitutions for Healthier Recipes

Whole Grains: Opt for whole grains like brown rice, quinoa, and whole wheat pasta instead of refined grains. They have a lower glycemic index and provide more fiber and nutrients.

Healthy Fats: Replace saturated fats with unsaturated fats like those found in olive oil, avocados, and nuts. These fats support heart health and help control blood sugar levels.

Natural Sweeteners: Use natural sweeteners like stevia or erythritol instead of refined sugars. These alternatives add sweetness without causing drastic spikes in blood sugar.

Lean Proteins: Choose lean protein sources such as skinless poultry, fish, tofu, and legumes. They are rich in essential nutrients and won't contribute to unhealthy cholesterol levels.

Low-Fat Dairy: Opt for low-fat or fat-free dairy products to reduce saturated fat intake. These options provide essential calcium and vitamin D without the added fat.

Portion Control: Be mindful of portion sizes. Even healthy foods can impact blood sugar if consumed excessively. Use smaller plates to help control portions and prevent overeating.

By incorporating these cooking techniques and making smart ingredient substitutions, you can create diabetes-friendly meals that are not only beneficial for your health but also a delight for your taste buds. Remember, small changes in the kitchen can lead to significant improvements in managing diabetes and overall well-being.

CHAPTER 2: 30-DAY MEAL PLAN

Day	Breakfast	Lunch	Snack	Dinner
Day 1	Scrambled Eggs with Spinach and Whole Grain Toast (310 kcal) [Page 20]	Creamy Mushroom Soup with Poached Egg (350 kcal) [Page 31]	Greek Yogurt with Honey and Granola (180 kcal) [Page 23]	Salmon with Pine Nuts (400 kcal) [Page 43]
Day 2	Whole Grain Oatmeal with Bananas and Almonds (330 kcal) [Page 21]	Quinoa and Black Bean Salad with Grilled Chicken (350 kcal) [Page 33]	Chia Pudding with Mango Purée and Orange (200 kcal) [Page 24]	Grilled Salmon with Vegetables (420 kcal) [Page 43]
Day 3	Greek Yogurt with Chia Seeds, Dried Apricots, and Almonds (290 kcal) [Page 23]	Light Chicken Broth with Vegetables (400 kcal) [Page 31]	Cinnamon and Walnut Biscotti (180 kcal) [Page 56]	Baked Fish with Quinoa and Vegetables (410 kcal) [Page 44]
Day 4	Flaxseed Porridge (280 kcal) [Page 22]	Turkey Medallions with Creamy Buckwheat & Spicy Vegetables (400 kcal) [Page 36]	Keto Almond Flour Croissants (210 kcal) [Page 56]	Chicken Rolls with Spinach, Feta (380 kcal) [Page 46]
Day 5	Vegetable Omelette with Whole Grain Avocado Toast (320 kcal) [Page 21]	Pasta with Mushrooms, Cherry Tomatoes, and Cheese (360 kcal) [Page 41]	Chia Avocado Pudding (310 kcal) [Page 57]	Pasta with Avocado-Lemon Sauce (370 kcal) [Page 47]
Day 6	Whole Grain Tiramisu Oatmeal with Raspberry Jam and Coffee Praline (350 kcal) [Page 22]	Gazpacho with Feta and Tomato Salsa (300 kcal) [Page 32]	Oat Bars with Nuts and Dried Fruits (230 kcal) [Page 61]	Seafood Medley Delight (440 kcal) [Page 45]
Day 7	Cheese Pancakes with Spinach and Parmesan Sauce (300 kcal) [Page 25]	Salmon with Celery Risotto and Wild Rice (480 kcal) [Page 40]	Homemade Fruit and Nut Candies (200 kcal) [Page 61]	Baked Chicken and Roasted Vegetable Salad (400 kcal) [Page 47]
Day 8	Pear, Ricotta, and Almond Tart (320 kcal) [Page 27]	Meatballs in Tomato Sauce (390 kcal) [Page 38]	Banana Berry Smoothie (220 kcal) [Page 24]	Baked Fish Tacos with Whole Grain Tortillas, Cabbage, and Avocado Salad (330 kcal) [Page 45]

Day	Breakfast	Lunch	Snack	Dinner
Day 9	Whole Grain Pancakes with Berries (310 kcal) [Page 26]	Crispy Chicken Schnitzel with Creamy Mashed Potatoes, Fresh Vegetables, and Yogurt Sauce (410 kcal) [Page 33]	Avocado Spinach Refresh Smoothie (200 kcal) [Page 28]	Seafood Medley Delight (340 kcal) [Page 45]
Day 10	Cottage Cheese and Berry Strudel (300 kcal) [Page 26]	Chicken Breast Stuffed with Spinach and Feta, Served with Grilled Vegetables (400 kcal) [Page 33]	Pear Cake with Honey and Almonds (260 kcal) [Page 59]	Pan-Fried Trout with Almond-Wine Sauce, Peas, and Quinoa (360 kcal) [Page 44]
Day 11	Whole Grain English Muffin with Peanut Butter and Sliced Apples (290 kcal) [Page 26]	Tender Chicken with Anchovies, Mushrooms, and Lemon-Nut Sauce (380 kcal) [Page 35]	Coconut Flour Muffins (240 kcal) [Page 60]	Grilled Shrimp with Tangy Marinade (320 kcal) [Page 88]
Day 12	Zucchini and Broccoli Fritters (310 kcal) [Page 29]	Turkey Cutlet with Poached Egg (370 kcal) [Page 36]	Light Sugar-Free Coffee Cheesecake (230 kcal) [Page 60]	Tuna Salad with Avocado and Crispy Chickpea Popcorn (310 kcal) [Page 40]
Day 13	Almond and Berry Cottage Cheese Bake (280 kcal) [Page 28]	Meat with Pumpkin in the Oven and Rice Side (360 kcal) [Page 37]	Chocolate Banana Bites (210 kcal) [Page 62]	Salmon Poke Bowl (350 kcal) [Page 98]
Day 14	Mushroom and Bell Pepper Frittata (290 kcal) [Page 28]	Grilled Chicken Salad with Mixed Greens, Tomatoes, and Vinaigrette (350 kcal) [Page 34]	Peanut Butter Cups (220 kcal) [Page 62]	Shrimp Caesar Salad (330 kcal) [Page 81]
Day 15	Whole Grain Waffles with Sugar-Free Syrup and Berries (320 kcal) [Page 25]	Rice with Julienne (400 kcal) [Page 35]	Lemon Tart (280 kcal) [Page 59]	Salmon with Pine Nuts (400 kcal) [Page 43]
Day 16	Flaxseed Porridge (280 kcal) [Page 22]	Lavash Rolls with Meat, Vegetables (390 kcal) [Page 37]	Zucchini Pancakes with Greek Yogurt, Tomato Salsa, and Sunflower Seeds (200 kcal) [Page 24]	Grilled Salmon with Vegetables (420 kcal) [Page 43]

Day	Breakfast	Lunch	Snack	Dinner
Day 17	Avocado Toast with Scrambled Eggs and Feta (310 kcal) [Page 21]	Turkey Patties with Light Yogurt Sauce (380 kcal) [Page 30]	Banana Chocolate Bites (210 kcal) [Page 58]	Cucumber Rolls with Salmon (350 kcal) [Page 43]
Day 18	Greek Yogurt Parfait with Granola and Fresh Berries (290 kcal) [Page 23]	Quiche Lorraine (370 kcal) [Page 39]	Coconut Flour Brownies (240 kcal) [Page 59]	Baked Fish with Quinoa and Vegetables (410 kcal) [Page 44]
Day 19	Chia Pudding with Mango Purée and Orange (270 kcal) [Page 24]	Meat and Crouton Salad (360 kcal) [Page 39]	Oat Baskets with Cottage Cheese and Berries (230 kcal) [Page 62]	Pan-Seared Tuna with Mango-Avocado Salsa (390 kcal) [Page 44]
Day 20	Banana Berry Smoothie (220 kcal) [Page 24]	Bean Medley Salad with Pan-Seared Shrimps (350 kcal) [Page 41]	Almond Cookies (220 kcal) [Page 63]	Sea Bass with Braised Sauerkraut (380 kcal) [Page 93]
Day 21	Cheesy Omelet with Green Onions and Tomatoes (320 kcal) [Page 29]	Warm Bowl with Brussels Sprouts, Lentil Mix, and Poached Egg (340 kcal) [Page 42]	Nut and Fruit Roll (210 kcal) [Page 63]	Greek-Style Sea Bass (370 kcal) [Page 94]
Day 22	Poached Eggs with Vegetables and Avocado on Whole Grain Toast (310 kcal) [Page 20]	Pasta with Artichokes and Spinach (420 kcal) [Page 41]	Mixed Berry and Kefir Wellness Smoothie (210 kcal) [Page 28]	Oven-Baked Trout Steaks (360 kcal) [Page 94]
Day 23	Flatbread with Gouda Cheese, Spinach, Cherry Tomatoes (290 kcal) [Page 27]	Spinach and Strawberry Salad with Grilled Chicken (340 kcal) [Page 34]	Avocado Spinach Refresh Smoothie (200 kcal) [Page 28]	Tuna Pasta with Vegetables and Olives (370 kcal) [Page 95]
Day 24	Banana Berry Smoothie (220 kcal) [Page 24]	Mushroom Chicken with Black Rice and Zucchini (360 kcal) [Page 34]	Pear Cake with Honey and Almonds (260 kcal) [Page 59]	Baked Dorada (Sea Bream) (350 kcal) [Page 95]
Day 25	Turkey Patties with Light Yogurt Sauce (300 kcal) [Page 30]	Grilled Vegetable Bowl with Quinoa (400 kcal) [Page 42]	Cottage Cheese Dessert with Berries (230 kcal) [Page 64]	New Year's Cod Skewers (340 kcal) [Page 96]

Day	Breakfast	Lunch	Snack	Dinner
Day 26	Zucchini Pancakes with Greek Yogurt, Tomato Salsa, and Sunflower Seeds (280 kcal) [Page 24]	Green Risotto with Seafood (380 kcal) [Page 39]	Fruit and Nut Bars with Seeds (250 kcal) [Page 60]	Cod Patties (330 kcal) [Page 96]
Day 27	Sunny-Side Up Eggs over Spinach and Feta (280 kcal) [Page 29]	Whole Wheat Turkey-Avocado Wrap (370 kcal) [Page 36]	Oat Cookies with Apples, Raisins, and Nuts (160 kcal) [Page 63]	Pangasius on a Vegetable Bed (320 kcal) [Page 97]
Day 28	Cheesy Omelet with Green Onions and Tomatoes (290 kcal) [Page 29]	Plov (400 kcal) [Page 37]	Grape Jelly with Whipped Cream (235kcal) [Page 57]	Seabass in Pesto Sauce with Vegetables (310 kcal) [Page 97]
Day 29	Avocado Spinach Refresh Smoothie (300 kcal) [Page 28]	Lentil and Vegetable Stew with Tofu (350 kcal) [Page 38]	Almond Cookies (220 kcal) [Page 63]	Fish Tagine (340 kcal) [Page 98]
Day 30	Chicken and Avocado Salad with Poached Eggs (380 kcal) [Page 30]	Grilled Vegetable Roll with Hummus (400 kcal) [Page 42]	Cottage Cheese Banana Ice Cream (230 kcal) [Page 64]	Salmon Poke Bowl (350 kcal) [Page 98]

Note: We wish to remind you that the 30-Day Meal Plan provided in this book is intended as a guide and a source of inspiration. The caloric content of the dishes is approximate and may vary depending on the portion sizes and specific ingredients. This plan represents a diverse, balanced menu, combining a richness of proteins, healthy fats, and minimal carbohydrates. It allows for following a low-carb diet while enjoying delicious and nutritious meals every day.

If you find that the calories in the recipes do not completely align with your personal needs or the plan, feel free to adjust the portion sizes. Increase or decrease them to ensure that the meal plan suits your individual goals and preferences. Be creative and enjoy each dish according to your needs!

CHAPTER 2: BREAKFAST

Scrambled Eggs with Spinach and Whole Grain Toast

Prep: 5 minutes | Cook: 0 minutes | Serves: 1

Ingredients:

- 4 large eggs
- 1 cup fresh spinach, chopped (about 30g)
- Salt and pepper, to taste
- 4 slices whole grain bread
- 1 tbsp olive oil (15ml)
- Fresh parsley, chopped (for garnish, optional)

Instructions:

1. Whisk eggs, season with salt and pepper.
2. Sauté chopped spinach in olive oil until wilted, about 2 minutes.
3. Pour whisked eggs into the skillet with spinach.
4. Cook, stirring gently, until eggs are fully scrambled and cooked to your preference.
5. Toast whole grain bread slices.
6. Divide scrambled eggs and spinach over toasted bread.
7. Garnish with chopped fresh parsley if desired.

Nutritional Information (Per Serving): calories: 320 | fat: 16g | protein: 20g | carbs: 26g | sugars: 3g | fiber: 5g | sodium: 480mg

Poached Eggs with Vegetables and Avocado on Whole Grain Toast

Prep: 5 minutes | Cook: 10 minutes | Serves: 1

Ingredients:

- 2 eggs
- 1/2 cup diced mixed vegetables (such as bell peppers, tomatoes, mushrooms, spinach) (about 75g)
- 1/2 ripe avocado, sliced (about 100g when sliced)
- 1 slice of whole grain bread, toasted
- Salt and pepper to taste
- Fresh herbs (such as dill or parsley), for garnish

Instructions:

1. Simmer water in a saucepan. Crack eggs into plastic wrap, wrap, and poach for 3-4 minutes.
2. Drain excess water.
3. Sauté mixed vegetables until tender, season with salt and pepper.
4. Place sautéed vegetables on toasted bread, top with poached eggs and sliced avocado.
5. Garnish with fresh herbs and black pepper.

Nutritional Information (Per Serving): Calories: 320 | Fat: 15g | Protein: 14g | Carbohydrates: 32g | Sugars: 4g | Fiber: 8g | Sodium: 320mg

Eggs Benedict with Turkey and Avocado on Toast with Hollandaise Sauce

Prep: 15 minutes | Cook: 10 minutes | Serves: 1

Ingredients:

- 1 whole grain English muffin, split and toasted
- 2 slices lean turkey breast
- 1/2 ripe avocado, sliced (about 100g when sliced)
- 2 poached eggs
- Fresh parsley, chopped
- Salt and pepper to taste

Hollandaise Sauce:
- 1 large egg yolk
- 1 teaspoon Dijon mustard
- 1 teaspoon lemon juice
- 3 tablespoons unsalted butter, melted (about 42g)
- Salt and cayenne pepper to taste

Instructions:

Prepare the Hollandaise sauce:

1. In a heatproof bowl, whisk together the egg yolk, Dijon mustard, and lemon juice.
2. Place the bowl over a pot of simmering water (double boiler) and whisk continuously until the mixture thickens slightly.
3. Slowly drizzle in the melted butter, whisking constantly, until the sauce thickens. Remove from

heat and season with salt and a pinch of cayenne pepper. Keep warm.

Assemble the Benedict:

1. On each toasted English muffin half, layer a slice of lean turkey breast, followed by sliced avocado.
2. Carefully place a poached egg on top of each avocado layer.
3. Spoon the warm Hollandaise sauce generously over the poached eggs.
4. Garnish with chopped fresh parsley, and season with salt and pepper to taste.

Nutritional Information (Per Serving): Calories: 400 | Fat: 22g | Protein: 28g | Carbohydrates: 26g | Sugars: 2g | Fiber: 5g | Sodium: 550mg

Avocado Toast with Scrambled Eggs and Feta

Prep: 5 minutes | Cook: 10 minutes | Serves: 1

Ingredients:

- 1 ripe avocado, mashed (about 200g when mashed)
- 2 large eggs, scrambled
- 2 tablespoons crumbled feta cheese (about 30g)
- 1 slice whole grain bread, toasted
- Fresh parsley, chopped (for garnish)
- Salt and pepper to taste

Instructions:

1. Spread mashed avocado evenly over the toasted whole grain bread.
2. Top with fluffy scrambled eggs and crumbled feta cheese.
3. Garnish with chopped fresh parsley and season with salt and pepper to taste.

Nutritional Information (Per Serving): Calories: 350 | Fat: 20g | Protein: 18g | Carbohydrates: 28g | Sugars: 3g | Fiber: 11g | Sodium: 450mg

Vegetable Omelette with Whole Grain Avocado Toast

Prep: 10 minutes | Cook: 10 minutes | Serves: 1

Ingredients:

- 2 large eggs
- 1/4 cup diced bell peppers (assorted colors) (about 37g)
- 1/4 cup diced tomatoes (37g)
- 1/4 cup diced onions (40g)
- Handful of fresh spinach or kale, chopped (about 30g for spinach, 35g for kale)
- 1/2 avocado, mashed (100g when mashed)
- 1 slice whole grain bread, toasted
- Fresh parsley or dill, chopped (for garnish)
- Salt and pepper to taste
- Cooking spray or olive oil for sautéing

Instructions:

1. Whisk eggs, season with salt and pepper.
2. Sauté bell peppers, tomatoes, and onions in a skillet until tender. Add spinach or kale, sauté briefly.
3. Pour whisked eggs over vegetables. Cook until set, then fold the omelette in half.
4. Spread mashed avocado on toasted whole grain bread.5. Place omelette alongside avocado toast. Garnish with fresh parsley or dill.

Nutritional Information (Per Serving): Calories: 320 | Fat: 18g | Protein: 18g | Carbohydrates: 25g | Sugars: 4g | Fiber: 10g | Sodium: 450mg

Whole Grain Oatmeal with Bananas and Almonds

Prep: 5 minutes | Cook: 5 minutes | Serves: 1

Ingredients:

- 1/2 cup whole grain oats (about 40g)
- 1 cup unsweetened almond milk (about 240ml)
- 1/4 teaspoon ground cinnamon (optional) (about 0.5g)
- 2 tablespoons chopped almonds (about 18g)
- 1 teaspoon honey or sugar-free syrup (optional) (about 7g for honey)
- 1 ripe banana, sliced (about 120g when sliced)

Instructions:

1. In a saucepan, bring the almond milk to a gentle boil over medium heat.
2. Stir in the whole grain oats and reduce the heat to low. Cook, stirring occasionally, for about 3-5 minutes or until the oats are creamy and tender.
3. Remove from heat and transfer the oatmeal to a serving bowl.
4. Top with sliced bananas, chopped almonds, and a drizzle of honey or sugar-free syrup if desired.
5. Sprinkle of ground cinnamon if you like.

Nutritional Information (Per Serving): Calories: 350 | Fat: 12g | Protein: 8g | Carbohydrates: 55g | Sugars: 18g | Fiber: 8g | Sodium: 180mg

Whole Grain Tiramisu Oatmeal with Raspberry Jam and Coffee Praline

Prep: 5 minutes | Cook: 5 minutes | Serves: 1

Ingredients:

- 1/2 cup whole grain oats (about 40g)
- 1 cup unsweetened almond milk (about 240ml)
- 1 tablespoon raspberry jam, sugar-free (about 20g)
- 1 teaspoon cocoa powder, unsweetened, for dusting (about 2-3g)
- 1 shot of espresso or 1/2 cup brewed coffee, unsweetened (about 30ml for espresso, 120ml for coffee)
- 1 tablespoon chopped nuts (such as almonds or hazelnuts), toasted (about 15g)

Instructions:

1. In a saucepan, bring the almond milk to a gentle boil over medium heat.
2. Stir in the whole grain oats and reduce the heat to low. Cook, stirring occasionally, for about 3-5 minutes or until the oats are creamy and tender.
3. Remove from heat and stir in the raspberry jam and freshly brewed espresso or coffee.
4. Transfer the oatmeal to a serving bowl.

5. Top with toasted chopped nuts and a dusting of unsweetened cocoa powder.

Nutritional Information (Per Serving): Calories: 320 | Fat: 12g | Protein: 8g | Carbohydrates: 48g | Sugars: 10g | Fiber: 8g | Sodium: 180mg

Flaxseed Porridge

Prep: 5 minutes | Cook: 5 minutes | Serves: 1

Ingredients:

- 1/2 cup flaxseeds (80g)
- 1 cup oat milk, unsweetened (240ml)
- 2 tbsp goji berries (20g)
- Fresh berries and mint leaves for garnish (amount varies as per taste)
- 1 tbsp mixed seeds (such as chia seeds, pumpkin seeds, sunflower seeds) (about 15g)
- 2 tablespoons date syrup or any other natural sweetener, if desired (about 30g for date syrup)

Instructions:

1. In a saucepan, combine flaxseeds and oat milk.
2. Bring to a gentle boil over medium heat, stirring continuously.
3. Reduce the heat to low and let the mixture simmer for 3-5 minutes until it thickens to your desired consistency. Stir in goji berries and mixed seeds.
4. Remove from heat and let it cool for a minute.
5. Drizzle with date syrup or any natural sweetener of your choice.
6. Transfer the porridge to a bowl and garnish with fresh berries and mint leaves.

Nutritional Information (Per Serving): Calories: 320 | Fat: 15g | Protein: 10g | Carbohydrates: 45g | Sugars: 18g | Fiber: 14g | Sodium: 70mg

Greek Yogurt with Honey and Granola

Prep: 5 minutes | Serves: 1

Ingredients:

- 1 cup low-fat Greek yogurt (about 245g)
- 1 tablespoon honey or a natural sugar substitute (about 21g for honey)
- 2 tablespoons granola, choose a variety low in added sugars (about 30g)
- Fresh berries or sliced fruits for topping (optional) (amount varies as per preference)

Instructions:

1. In a bowl, scoop the Greek yogurt.
2. Drizzle the honey over the yogurt.
3. Sprinkle the granola on top.
4. If desired, add fresh berries or sliced fruits for extra flavor and nutrition.

Nutritional Information (Per Serving): Calories: 250 | Fat: 8g | Protein: 20g | Carbohydrates: 28g | Sugars: 18g | Fiber: 2g | Sodium: 50mg

Greek Yogurt with Chia Seeds, Dried Apricots, and Almonds

Prep: 5 minutes | Serves: 1

Ingredients:

- 1 cup of low-fat Greek yogurt (about 245g)
- 1 tablespoon chia seeds (about 10-15g)
- 2 tablespoons chopped unsweetened dried apricots (about 30g)
- 1 tablespoon chopped almonds (about 15g)

Instructions:

1. In a bowl, mix Greek yogurt and chia seeds. Stir well and let it sit overnight to allow the chia seeds to absorb moisture and thicken the yogurt.
2. Add the chopped dried apricots to the mixture.

3. Sprinkle the yogurt with chopped almonds for a delightful crunch.

Nutritional Information (Per Serving): Calories: 300 | Fat: 12g | Protein: 20g | Carbohydrates: 30g | Sugars: 15g | Fiber: 9g | Sodium: 60mg

Greek Yogurt Parfait with Granola and Fresh Berries

Prep: 10 minutes | Serves: 1

Ingredients:

- 1/4 cup granola, unsweetened and low-carb if available (about 60g)
- 1/2 cup fresh mixed berries, such as strawberries, blueberries, and raspberries (about 75g)
- 1 teaspoon honey or a sugar-free sweetener (optional, depending on sweetness preference) (about 7g for honey)
- Fresh mint leaves for garnish (optional) (amount varies as per taste)
- 1 cup low-fat Greek yogurt (about 245g)

Instructions:

1. In a glass or a bowl, layer half of the Greek yogurt at the bottom.
2. Add a layer of fresh mixed berries on top of the yogurt.
3. Sprinkle half of the granola over the berries.
4. Repeat the layers with the remaining yogurt, berries, and granola.
5. Drizzle honey over the top for added sweetness if desired.
6. Garnish with fresh mint leaves for a refreshing touch.

Nutritional Information (Per Serving): Calories: 300 | Fat: 8g | Protein: 18g | Carbohydrates: 42g | Sugars: 22g | Fiber: 6g | Sodium: 80mg

Chia Pudding with Mango Purée and Orange

Prep: 10 minutes | Serves: 1

Ingredients:

- 1/4 cup chia seeds (42g)
- 1 cup unsweetened almond milk (or any other preferred milk) (about 240ml)
- 1 ripe mango, peeled and pitted (about 200g of edible part)
- 1 orange, peeled and segmented (about 130g of edible part)
- 1 tbsp honey or a sugar-free sweetener (optional) (21g for honey)
- Fresh mint leaves for garnish (optional)

Instructions:

1. In a bowl, combine chia seeds and almond milk. Stir well to avoid clumps. Let it sit in the refrigerator for at least 2 hours or overnight, allowing the chia seeds to absorb the liquid and create a pudding-like consistency.
2. In a blender, puree the ripe mango until smooth.
3. In serving glasses or bowls, layer the chia pudding and mango puree. Start with a layer of chia pudding, followed by a layer of mango puree, and repeat.
4. Top the layers with fresh orange segments and garnish with fresh mint leaves for a refreshing touch.

Nutritional Information (Per Serving): Calories: 180 | Fat: 7g | Protein: 4g | Carbohydrates: 28g | Sugars: 18g | Fiber: 10g | Sodium: 70mg

Banana Berry Smoothie

Prep: 5 minutes | Serves: 1

Ingredients:

- 1 ripe banana, peeled and sliced (120g when sliced)
- 1/2 cup mixed berries (such as strawberries, blueberries, and raspberries), fresh or frozen (about 75g)
- 1/2 cup unsweetened almond milk (or any other preferred milk) (120ml)
- 1/2 cup plain low-fat Greek yogurt (about 120g)
- 1 tablespoon chopped hazelnuts (about 15g)

Instructions:

1. In a blender, combine the sliced banana, mixed berries, chopped hazelnuts, almond milk, Greek yogurt.
2. Blend until smooth and creamy. If the smoothie is too thick, you can add a little more almond milk or water to reach your desired consistency.
3. If preferred, add a handful of ice cubes and blend again until the smoothie is chilled and refreshing.
4. Pour the smoothie into a glass and garnish with a few whole berries and a sprinkle of chopped hazelnuts.

Nutritional Information (Per Serving): Calories: 280 | Fat: 10g | Protein: 14g | Carbohydrates: 39g | Sugars: 21g | Fiber: 7g | Sodium: 80mg

Zucchini Pancakes with Greek Yogurt, Tomato Salsa, and Sunflower Seeds

Prep: 15 minutes | Cook: 10 minutes | Serves: 2

Ingredients:

- 2 medium zucchinis, grated (about 500g total)
- 1 cup fresh spinach, chopped (about 30g)
- 1/4 cup whole wheat flour (about 30g)
- 2 tablespoons roasted sunflower seeds (18g)
- 1 egg, beaten
- Salt and pepper to taste
- 1 tablespoon olive oil, for cooking (about 15ml)
- 1/2 cup plain low-fat Greek yogurt (about 120g)
- 1/2 cup fresh tomato salsa (about 120g)
- 1/4 cup grated Parmesan cheese (about 25g)

Instructions:

1. In a large bowl, combine grated zucchinis, chopped spinach, whole wheat flour, Parmesan cheese, beaten egg, salt, and pepper. Mix well until all ingredients are combined.
2. Heat olive oil in a non-stick skillet over medium heat. Scoop spoonfuls of the zucchini mixture onto the skillet, flattening them with the back of the spoon. Cook for 3-4 minutes on each side or until

golden brown and cooked through. Remove from the skillet and set aside.

3. In a small bowl, mix Greek yogurt with fresh tomato salsa.

4. Serve the zucchini pancakes topped with a dollop of the yogurt and salsa mixture. Sprinkle roasted sunflower seeds on top.

Nutritional Information (Per Serving): Calories: 280 | Fat: 14g | Protein: 16g | Carbohydrates: 25g | Sugars: 8g | Fiber: 6g | Sodium: 420mg

Cheese Pancakes with Spinach and Parmesan Sauce

Prep: 15 minutes | Cook: 10 minutes | Serves: 2

Ingredients:

- 1 cup fresh spinach, finely chopped (about 30g)
- 1 cup cottage cheese, low-fat (about 226g)
- 1/4 cup whole wheat flour (about 30g)
- 1/4 cup grated Parmesan cheese (about 25g)
- 1 egg, beaten

  For Parmesan Sauce:
- 1/2 cup low-fat sour cream (about 115g)
- Salt and pepper to taste
- 1 tbsp olive oil, for cooking (about 15ml)
- 8 oz mild smoked salmon, thinly sliced (225g)
- 1/2 cup sun-dried tomatoes, rehydrated and sliced (about 54g)
- 1 tbsp fresh lemon juice (about 15ml)
- Salt and pepper to taste
- 1/4 cup grated Parmesan cheese (about 25g)

Instructions:

1. In a mixing bowl, combine chopped spinach, cottage cheese, whole wheat flour, grated Parmesan cheese, beaten egg, salt, and pepper. Mix until well combined.

2. Heat olive oil in a non-stick skillet over medium heat. Spoon the batter onto the skillet, forming pancakes. Cook for 3-4 minutes on each side or until golden brown and cooked through. Remove from the skillet and set aside.

3. In a small bowl, whisk together low-fat sour cream, grated Parmesan cheese, fresh lemon juice, salt, and pepper to create the Parmesan sauce.

4. Serve the spinach cheese pancakes topped with Parmesan sauce, mild smoked salmon slices, and rehydrated sun-dried tomatoes.

Nutritional Information (Per Serving): Calories: 420 | Fat: 22g | Protein: 30g | Carbohydrates: 25g | Sugars: 6g | Fiber: 4g | Sodium: 720mg

Whole Grain Waffles with Sugar-Free Syrup and Berries

Prep: 10 minutes | Cook: 15 minutes | Serves: 2

Ingredients:

- 1 cup whole wheat flour (about 120g)
- 1 teaspoon baking powder (about 4g)
- 1/2 teaspoon cinnamon (about 1.5g)
- 1 cup unsweetened almond milk (or any preferred milk) (about 240ml)
- 1 egg, beaten
- 1 tablespoon olive oil (about 15ml)
- Sugar-free syrup, for serving (amount varies as per taste)
- Fresh mixed berries, for topping (amount varies as per preference)

Instructions:

1. In a mixing bowl, combine whole wheat flour, baking powder, and cinnamon.

2. Add almond milk, beaten egg, and olive oil to the dry ingredients. Mix until well combined.

3. Preheat your waffle iron. Pour the batter onto the hot waffle iron and cook until golden and crispy.

4. Serve the whole grain waffles with sugar-free syrup and a generous topping of fresh mixed berries.

Nutritional Information (Per Serving): Calories: 320 | Fat: 10g | Protein: 9g | Carbohydrates: 50g | Sugars: 6g | Fiber: 9g | Sodium: 280mg

Whole Grain Pancakes with Berries

Prep: 10 minutes | Cook: 15 minutes | Serves: 2

Ingredients:

- 1 cup whole wheat flour (about 120g)
- 1 tablespoon baking powder (about 14g)
- 1/2 teaspoon cinnamon (about 1.5g)
- 1 cup unsweetened almond milk (or any preferred milk) (about 240ml)
- 1 egg, beaten
- 1 tablespoon olive oil (about 15ml)
- Fresh mixed berries, for topping (amount varies as per preference)
- Sugar-free syrup, for serving (amount varies as per taste)

Instructions:

1. In a mixing bowl, combine whole wheat flour, baking powder, and cinnamon.
2. Add almond milk, beaten egg, and olive oil to the dry ingredients. Mix until well combined.
3. Heat a non-stick skillet over medium heat and lightly grease it.
4. Pour a small amount of batter onto the skillet to form each pancake. Cook until bubbles form on the surface, then flip and cook until golden brown on the other side.
5. Serve the whole grain pancakes with a generous topping of fresh mixed berries and a drizzle of sugar-free syrup.

Nutritional Information (Per Serving): Calories: 280 | Fat: 8g | Protein: 10g | Carbohydrates: 45g | Sugars: 5g | Fiber: 7g | Sodium: 320mg

Whole Grain English Muffin with Peanut Butter and Sliced Apples

Prep: 5 minutes | Cook: 5 minutes | Serves: 1

Ingredients:

- 1 whole grain English muffin, split and toasted
- 1/2 medium apple, thinly sliced (about 55g)
- 2 tablespoons natural peanut butter (no added sugar or oil) (about 32g)

Instructions:

1. Spread the natural peanut butter evenly over the toasted English muffin halves.
2. Arrange the thinly sliced apples on top of the peanut butter layer.
3. Close the muffin halves to make a sandwich.

Nutritional Information (Per Serving): Calories: 320 | Fat: 14g | Protein: 10g | Carbohydrates: 44g | Sugars: 12g | Fiber: 10g | Sodium: 310mg

Cottage Cheese and Berry Strudel

Prep: 15 minutes | Cook: 25 minutes | Serves: 6

Ingredients:

- 6 sheets phyllo pastry
- 1 cup low-fat cottage cheese (240 ml)
- 1 cup mixed berries (such as raspberries, blueberries, and strawberries), fresh or frozen (240 ml)
- 2 tablespoons honey or a sugar-free sweetener (approximately 30 g)
- 2 tbsp chopped almonds (approximately 20 g)
- Cooking spray

Instructions:

1. Preheat oven to 350°F (175°C).
2. Mix cottage cheese, mixed berries, and honey in a bowl.
3. Stack 3 sheets of phyllo, spray with cooking spray. Spoon filling along one edge, roll to form a strudel.
4. Place strudel on parchment-lined baking sheet, spray the top, sprinkle with almonds. Bake for 25 minutes until golden and crispy.

Nutritional Information (Per Serving): Calories: 180 | Fat: 5g | Protein: 8g | Carbohydrates: 27g | Sugars: 11g | Fiber: 3g | Sodium: 210mg

Pear, Ricotta, and Almond Tart

Prep: 15 minutes | Cook: 30 minutes | Serves: 8

Ingredients:

- 1 sheet whole wheat puff pastry, thawed
- 1/2 cup low-fat ricotta cheese (120 ml)
- 2 ripe pears, thinly sliced
- 2 tbsp chopped almonds (30 g)
- 1 tbsp honey or a sugar-free sweetener (15 ml)
- 1/2 tsp ground cinnamon

Instructions:

1. Preheat the oven to 375°F (190°C).
2. Roll out the puff pastry sheet into a rectangular shape and transfer it to a baking sheet lined with parchment paper.
3. Spread the low-fat ricotta cheese evenly over the puff pastry, leaving a border around the edges.
4. Arrange the thinly sliced pears on top of the ricotta cheese. Drizzle with honey and sprinkle with chopped almonds and ground cinnamon.
5. Bake for 25-30 minutes or until the pastry is golden brown and the pears are tender.
6. Allow the tart to cool slightly before slicing and serving.

Nutritional Information (Per Serving): Calories: 180 | Fat: 8g | Protein: 4g | Carbohydrates: 24g | Sugars: 10g | Fiber: 4g | Sodium: 120mg

Hawaiian Pizza

Prep: 15 minutes | Cook: 15 minutes | Serves: 4

Ingredients:

- 1 whole wheat pizza crust (store-bought or homemade)
- 1/2 cup low-sodium tomato sauce (about 120ml)
- 1-2 tomatoes, sliced (180g for one medium tomato)
- 1 cup chopped cooked chicken (about 140g)
- 1/2 cup pineapple chunks, fresh or canned in juice, drained (about 82g)
- 1/2 cup shredded part-skim mozzarella cheese (56g)
- 1/2 cup chopped olives (67g)
- 1/4 teaspoon black pepper
- Fresh basil leaves for garnish (optional)

Instructions:

1. Preheat the oven to 450°F (230°C).
2. Roll out the pizza crust on a baking sheet or pizza stone.
3. Spread the tomato sauce evenly over the crust, leaving a slight border around the edges. Place tomato slices on top.
4. Top with diced chicken, pineapple pieces, shredded mozzarella, and chopped olives. Season with black pepper.
5. Bake the pizza in the preheated oven for 12 to 15 minutes or until the crust is golden brown and the cheese is melted and bubbly.
6. Remove from the oven, let it cool for a minute, garnish with fresh basil if desired, slice, and serve.

Nutritional Information (Per Serving): Calories: 320 | Fat: 10g | Protein: 20g | Carbohydrates: 38g | Sugars: 7g | Fiber: 6g | Sodium: 480mg

Flatbread with Gouda Cheese, Spinach, Cherry Tomatoes

Prep: 10 minutes | Cook: 5 minutes | Serves: 2

Ingredients:

- 2 whole grain lavash wraps
- 1 cup shredded Gouda cheese (about 113g)
- 1 cup fresh spinach leaves (about 30g)
- 1/2 cup cherry tomatoes, halved (90g)
- 2 tbsp flaxseeds (20g)
- Black pepper, to taste

Instructions:

1. Preheat oven to 350°F (175°C).
2. Place lavash wraps on a baking sheet. Sprinkle Gouda cheese, spinach, and cherry tomatoes evenly. Sprinkle flaxseeds and black pepper.
3. Bake for 5-7 minutes until lavash is crispy, and cheese is melted.
4. Remove from oven, slice, and serve immediately.

Nutritional Information (Per Serving): Calories: 290 | Fat: 14g | Protein: 14g | Carbohydrates: 28g | Sugars: 2g | Fiber: 12g | Sodium: 320mg

Mixed Berry and Kefir Wellness Smoothie

Prep: 5 minutes | Cook: 0 minutes | Serves: 1

Ingredients:

- 1 cup mixed berries (strawberries, blueberries, raspberries) (140g)
- 1 cup plain kefir (240ml)
- 1 tbsp chia seeds (15g)
- 1/2 tsp vanilla extract
- A pinch of cinnamon

Instructions:

1. Place berries, kefir, chia seeds, vanilla extract, and cinnamon in a blender.
2. Blend until smooth.
3. Serve chilled.

Nutritional Information (Per Serving): Calories: 258.3 | Fat: 10.4g | Carbohydrates: 34.9g | Protein: 11.9g | Fiber: 8.5g | Sugars: 24.0g | Sodium: 124.0mg

Avocado Spinach Refresh Smoothie

Prep: 5 minutes | Cook: 0 minutes | Serves: 1

Ingredients:

- 1 ripe avocado (150g)
- 1 cup fresh spinach (30g)
- 1/2 cup unsweetened almond milk (120ml)
- 1/2 cup Greek yogurt (120g)
- Juice of 1/2 lemon
- Ice cubes

Instructions:

1. Combine avocado, spinach, almond milk, Greek yogurt, and lemon juice in a blender.
2. Add a handful of ice cubes and blend until smooth.
3. Serve immediately.

Nutritional Information (Per Serving): Calories: 336.6 | Fat: 24.5g | Carbohydrates: 20.1g | Protein: 16.4g | Fiber: 11.2g | Sugars: 5.9g | Sodium: 257.5mg

Mushroom and Bell Pepper Frittata

Prep: 10 minutes | Cook: 15 minutes | Serves: 2

Ingredients:

- 4 large eggs (50g each)
- 1/2 cup sliced mushrooms (75g)
- 1/2 red bell pepper, diced (75g)
- 1/4 cup shredded cheese (30g) (optional)
- 1 tbsp olive oil (15ml)
- Salt and pepper to taste
- Fresh herbs (parsley, chives) for garnish

Instructions:

1. In a skillet, heat olive oil over medium heat. Sauté mushrooms and bell pepper until soft.
2. Beat eggs in a bowl and season with salt and pepper.
3. Pour eggs into the skillet. Cook until the bottom is set but the top is still slightly runny.
4. Sprinkle with cheese and cover. Let cook until cheese melts and eggs are fully set.
5. Garnish with fresh herbs before serving.

Nutritional Information (Per Serving): Calories: 301.5 | Fat: 23.7g | Carbohydrates: 4.8g | Protein: 18.3g | Fiber: 1.2g | Sugars: 3.5g | Sodium: 220.7mg

Almond and Berry Cottage Cheese Bake

Prep: 10 minutes | Cook: 25 minutes | Serves: 2

Ingredients:

- 1 cup cottage cheese (225g)
- 1/2 cup mixed berries (raspberries, blueberries) (70g)
- 1/4 cup sliced almonds (30g)
- 2 tbsp almond flour (15g)
- 1 tbsp honey (optional) (15ml)
- 1/2 tsp vanilla extract

Instructions:

1. Preheat oven to 375°F (190°C).
2. In a bowl, mix cottage cheese with vanilla extract and honey (if using).
3. Fold in berries and almond flour.

4. Pour the mixture into a baking dish. Sprinkle with sliced almonds.

5. Bake for 25 minutes or until set and lightly golden. Serve warm.

Nutritional Information (Per Serving): Calories: 287.7 | Fat: 16.6g | Carbohydrates: 19.7g | Protein: 17.6g | Fiber: 3.4g | Sugars: 13.8g | Sodium: 411.2mg

Zucchini and Broccoli Fritters

Prep: 15 minutes | Cook: 10 minutes | Serves: 2

Ingredients:

- 1 cup grated zucchini (120g)
- 1 cup chopped broccoli (90g)
- 2 large eggs
- 1/4 cup almond flour (30g)
- 1/4 tsp garlic powder
- Salt and pepper to taste
- Olive oil for cooking

Instructions:

1. Squeeze excess moisture from grated zucchini.
2. In a bowl, mix zucchini, broccoli, eggs, almond flour, garlic powder, salt, and pepper.
3. Heat oil in a skillet over medium heat.
4. Scoop the mixture into the skillet, flatten to form fritters.
5. Cook until golden brown, about 3-4 minutes per side. Serve hot.

Nutritional Information (Per Serving): Calories: 193.2 | Fat: 13.8g | Carbohydrates: 8.7g | Protein: 11.7g | Fiber: 3.3g | Sugars: 3.5g | Sodium: 83.5mg

Cheesy Omelet with Green Onions and Tomatoes

Prep: 5 minutes | Cook: 10 minutes | Serves: 1

Ingredients:

- 2 large eggs
- 1/4 cup chopped tomatoes (40g)
- 1/4 cup chopped green onions (25g)
- 1/4 cup shredded cheese (such as cheddar or mozzarella) (30g)
- Salt and pepper to taste
- Butter for cooking

Instructions:

1. Beat eggs with salt and pepper.
2. Melt butter in a skillet over medium heat.
3. Pour in the eggs. Once they begin to set, sprinkle tomatoes, green onions, and cheese.
4. Fold the omelet in half and cook until cheese melts. Serve warm.

Nutritional Information (Per Serving): Calories: 290.8 | Fat: 21.0g | Carbohydrates: 4.9g | Protein: 21.3g | Fiber: 1.1g | Sugars: 2.8g | Sodium: 316.3mg

Sunny-Side Up Eggs over Spinach and Feta

Prep:5 minutes | Cook: 10 minutes | Serves: 1

Ingredients:

- 2 large eggs (100g)
- 2 cups fresh spinach (60g)
- 1/4 cup feta cheese, crumbled (50g)
- 1 tbsp olive oil (15ml)
- Salt and pepper to taste

Instructions:

1. Heat olive oil in a skillet over medium heat.
2. Add spinach and cook until wilted, about 2-3 minutes.
3. Sprinkle feta cheese over the spinach.
4. Carefully crack eggs over the spinach and feta. Season with salt and pepper.
5. Cover and cook until the egg whites are set but yolks are still runny, about 5 minutes.
6. Serve immediately.

Nutritional Information (Per Serving): Calories: 300 | Fat: 36.7g | Carbohydrates: 5.3g | Protein: 21.7g | Fiber: 1.3g | Sugars: 3.3g | Sodium: 729.7mg

Chicken and Avocado Salad with Poached Eggs

Prep: 15 minutes | Cook: 10 minutes | Serves: 2

Ingredients:

- 2 poached eggs (100g)
- 2 cups mixed salad greens (60g)
- 1 grilled chicken breast, sliced (150g)
- 1 ripe avocado, sliced (150g)
- 2 tbsp olive oil (30ml)
- 1 tbsp balsamic vinegar (15ml)
- Salt and pepper to taste

Instructions:

1. Arrange mixed greens on two plates.
2. Top with sliced grilled chicken and avocado.
3. Poach eggs to your preference.
4. Place a poached egg on top of each salad.
5. Drizzle with olive oil and balsamic vinegar.
6. Season with salt and pepper to taste.
7. Serve immediately.

Nutritional Information (Per Serving): Calories: 380 | Fat: 33.8g | Carbohydrates: 9.5g | Protein: 32.0g | Fiber: 5.9g | Sugars: 2.1g | Sodium: 156.5mg

Baked Egg Cups with Cottage Cheese and Greens

Prep: 10 minutes | Cook: 15 minutes | Serves: 2

Ingredients:

- 4 large eggs (200g)
- 1/2 cup cottage cheese (115g)
- 1 cup chopped kale or spinach (30g)
- Salt and pepper to taste
- Cooking spray or oil for greasing

Instructions:

1. Preheat oven to 375°F (190°C). Grease a muffin tin with cooking spray or oil.
2. Divide chopped kale or spinach and cottage cheese evenly among 4 muffin cups.

3. Crack an egg into each cup.
4. Season with salt and pepper.
5. Bake for 15 minutes or until eggs are set to your liking.
6. Let cool for a minute, then carefully remove from the tin.
7. Serve warm.

Nutritional Information (Per Serving): Calories: 230 | Fat: 13.6g | Carbohydrates: 4.4g | Protein: 20.0g | Fiber: 0.5g | Sugars: 2.7g | Sodium: 344.7mg

Turkey Patties with Light Yogurt Sauce

Prep: 20 minutes | Cook: 15 minutes | Serves: 4

Ingredients:

- 1 pound ground turkey (450g)
- 1/4 cup finely chopped onion (40g)
- 2 cloves garlic, minced (6g)
- 1 tsp dried oregano
- 1/2 tsp paprika
- Salt and pepper to taste
- 1 cup Greek yogurt (240g)
- 1 tbsp lemon juice (15ml)
- 1 tbsp chopped fresh dill (4g)
- Olive oil for cooking

Instructions:

1. In a bowl, combine ground turkey, onion, garlic, oregano, paprika, salt, and pepper. Mix well.
2. Form the mixture into small patties.
3. Heat a drizzle of olive oil in a skillet over medium heat. Cook the patties for about 6-7 minutes on each side or until cooked through.
4. For the sauce, mix Greek yogurt with lemon juice and dill. Season with salt and pepper.
5. Serve the turkey patties with the yogurt sauce on the side.

Nutritional Information (Per Serving): Calories: 250 | Fat: 11.5g | Carbohydrates: 3.9g | Protein: 36.6g | Fiber: 0.2g | Sugars: 2.7g | Sodium: 107.3mg

CHAPTER 3: LUNCH

Creamy Mushroom Soup with Poached Egg

Prep: 10 minutes | Cook: 25 minutes | Serves: 4

Ingredients:

- 1 cup chopped mushrooms (about 70g)
- 1 small onion, finely chopped (about 70g)
- 2 cloves garlic, minced (about 6g)
- 1/2 cup low-fat milk (about 120ml)
- Salt and pepper to taste
- 1 poached egg (optional)
- 2 cups vegetable broth (about 480ml)

Instructions:

1. In a saucepan, fry mushrooms, onions and garlic until tender.
2. Add vegetable broth and bring to a boil. Simmer for 10 minutes.
3. Using an immersion blender, puree the soup until smooth.
4. Add low-fat milk, salt and pepper. Cook for another 5 minutes.
5. Serve hot, garnished with a poached egg (optional) and chopped fresh parsley.

Nutritional Information (Per Serving): Calories: 150 | Fat: 2.3g | Protein: 3.6g | Carbohydrates: 5.4g | Sugars: 3.2g | Fiber: 0.5g | Sodium: 1062.5mg.

Tomato Lentil Soup with Salad

Prep: 15 minutes | Cook: 25 minutes | Serves: 4

Ingredients:

- 1 cup red lentils, rinsed (about 200g)
- 1 onion, chopped (150g)
- 2 tomatoes, diced (240g)
- 1 carrot, diced (about 61g)
- 4 cups chicken broth (960ml)
- 1 teaspoon ground cumin
- Salt and pepper to taste
- Freshly squeezed lemon juice for garnish (amount varies as per taste)
- Fresh mint leaves, chopped, for garnish (amount varies as per preference)

Instructions:

1. Soak the lentils in cold water for 2-3 hours.
2. In a saucepan, combine lentils, onions, tomatoes, carrots and vegetable broth. Bring to the boil, then simmer for 20 minutes or until the lentils are tender.
3. Using a blender, puree the soup until smooth. Season with cumin, salt and pepper.
4. Serve hot, garnished with fresh lemon juice and chopped mint leaves.

Nutritional Information (Per Serving): Calories: 220 | Fat: 0.9g | Carbohydrates: 19.5g | Protein: 5.8g | Fiber: 5.8g | Sugars: 5.4g | Sodium: 2080.0mg

Light Chicken Broth with Vegetables

Prep: 15 minutes | Cook: 25 minutes | Serves: 4

Ingredients:

- 1 lb boneless, skinless chicken breast, cooked and shredded (about 454g)
- 4 cups low-sodium chicken broth (about 960ml)
- 1 cup spinach, chopped (about 30g)
- 1/2 cup kidney beans, cooked (about 90g)
- 1 carrot, diced (about 61g)
- 1 small onion, finely chopped (about 70g)
- 2 cloves garlic, minced (6g)
- 1 quail egg, boiled (optional) (about 9g per egg)
- Salt and pepper to taste
- Fresh parsley, chopped, for garnish (amount varies as per preference)

Instructions:

1. In a pot, sauté onions and garlic until translucent.
2. Add carrots and continue cooking for 2 minutes.
3. Pour in chicken broth and bring to a boil. Add shredded chicken, spinach, and kidney beans. Simmer for 10-15 minutes.

4. Season with salt and pepper. Garnish with a boiled quail egg (if using) and fresh parsley before serving.

Nutritional Information (Per Serving): Calories: 220 | Fat: 5.5g | Carbohydrates: 11.2g | Protein: 42.4g | Fiber: 2.4g | Sugars: 2.5g | Sodium: 273.0mg

Gazpacho with Feta and Tomato Salsa

Prep: 15 minutes | Chill: 1 hour | Cook: 0 minutes | Serves: 4

Ingredients:

- 4 large ripe tomatoes, diced (about 900g total)
- 1 cucumber, peeled and diced (about 300g)
- 1 red bell pepper, chopped (about 150g)
- 1 small red onion, finely chopped (about 70g)
- 2 cloves garlic, minced (about 6g)
- 1/4 cup fresh basil, chopped (about 15g)
- 1/4 cup fresh parsley, chopped (about 15g)
- 1/2 cup feta cheese, crumbled (about 75g)
- 2 tablespoons olive oil (30ml)
- 3 cups tomato juice (720ml)
- Salt and pepper to taste

Instructions:

1. In a large bowl, combine diced tomatoes, cucumber, bell pepper, red onion, and garlic.
2. Pour in tomato juice and olive oil. Add basil and parsley. Season with salt and pepper. Mix well.
3. Chill the gazpacho in the refrigerator for at least 1 hour to let the flavors meld.
4. Serve cold, garnished with crumbled feta cheese.

Nutritional Information (Per Serving): Calories: 180 | Fat: 13.1g | Carbohydrates: 15.8g | Protein: 6.3g | Fiber: 2.5g | Sugars: 9.3g | Sodium: 332.0mg

Summer Cold Tomato and Pepper Soup with Whole Grain Chips, Nuts, and Seeds

Prep: 15 minutes | Chill: 1 hour | Cook: 0 minutes | Serves: 4

Ingredients:

- 6 ripe tomatoes, diced (about 900g total)
- 2 bell peppers (any color), chopped (about 300g total)
- 1 cucumber, peeled and diced (about 300g)
- 1 small red onion, finely chopped (about 70g)
- 2 cloves garlic, minced (about 6g)
- 4 cups low-sodium vegetable broth (about 960ml)
- 1/4 cup fresh basil, chopped (about 15g)
- 1/4 cup fresh parsley, chopped (about 15g)
- Salt and pepper to taste
- Whole grain chips, nuts, and seeds for garnish (amount varies as per preference)

Instructions:

1. In a blender, combine tomatoes, bell peppers, cucumber, red onion, and garlic. Blend until smooth.
2. Pour the mixture into a large bowl. Stir in vegetable broth, basil, and parsley. Season with salt and pepper.
3. Chill the soup in the refrigerator for at least 1 hour.
4. Serve cold, garnished with whole grain chips, nuts, and seeds for added texture.

Nutritional Information (Per Serving): Calories: 150 | Fat: 1.8g | Carbohydrates: 20.6g | Protein: 8.1g | Fiber: 5.2g | Sugars: 12.0g | Sodium: 187.0mg

Crispy Chicken Schnitzel with Creamy Mashed Potatoes, Fresh Vegetables, and Yogurt Sauce

Prep: 20 minutes | Cook: 20 minutes | Serves: 4

Ingredients:

- 4 boneless, skinless chicken breasts (150-200g each)
- 1/2 cup whole wheat flour (about 60g)
- 2 eggs, beaten
- 1 cup whole grain breadcrumbs (about 120g)
- 1 teaspoon paprika
- Salt and pepper to taste
- 1/2 cup plain Greek yogurt (about 120g)
- 4 medium potatoes, peeled, boiled, and mashed with 1/4 cup grated Parmesan cheese (each potato approximately 150g before peeling, and about 25g for Parmesan)
- Mixed fresh vegetables (e.g., broccoli, carrots), steamed (amount varies as per preference)
- Fresh dill, chopped, for garnish (amount varies as per preference)

Instructions:

1. Preheat the oven to 375°F (190°C). Line a baking sheet with parchment paper.
2. Season the chicken breasts with salt, pepper, and paprika. Dredge each chicken breast in flour, then dip in beaten eggs, and coat with whole grain breadcrumbs.
3. Place the breaded chicken breasts on the prepared baking sheet. Bake for 18-20 minutes or until golden and crispy.
4. While the chicken is baking, prepare the mashed potatoes by boiling and mashing the potatoes. Stir in grated Parmesan cheese.
5. Serve the crispy chicken with creamy mashed potatoes, steamed vegetables, and a side of yogurt sauce garnished with fresh dill.

Nutritional Information (Per Serving): Calories: 380 | Fat: 13.1g | Carbohydrates: 59.4g | Protein: 71.9g | Fiber: 7.1g | Sugars: 4.9g | Sodium: 471.6mg

Chicken Breast Stuffed with Spinach and Feta, Served with Grilled Vegetables

Prep: 15 minutes | Cook: 20 minutes | Serves: 4

Ingredients:

- 4 boneless, skinless chicken breasts (150-200g each)
- 2 cups fresh spinach, chopped (about 60g)
- 1/2 cup crumbled feta cheese (about 75g)
- 2 tbsp olive oil (30ml)
- 1 tsp garlic powder
- Salt and pepper to taste
- Mixed vegetables for grilling (e.g., bell peppers, zucchini, cherry tomatoes) (amount varies as per preference)
- Fresh lemon wedges for serving (amount varies as per preference)

Instructions:

1. Heat grill or pan on medium.
2. Slice pockets in chicken breasts. Season inside with garlic, salt, and pepper. Stuff with spinach and feta. Secure with toothpicks.
3. Brush chicken with olive oil. Grill 10-12 minutes each side until done.
4. Season vegetables with olive oil, salt, and pepper. Grill until tender.
5. Remove toothpicks from chicken. Serve with vegetables and lemon wedges.

Nutritional Information (Per Serving): Calories: 320 | Fat: 17.8g | Carbohydrates: 1.5g | Protein: 57.4g | Fiber: 0.4g |Sugars: 0.8g |Sodium: 350.9mg

Quinoa and Black Bean Salad with Grilled Chicken

Prep: 15 minutes | Cook: 15 minutes | Serves: 4

Ingredients:

- 1 cup quinoa, cooked and cooled (185g when cooked)
- 1 can (15 oz) black beans, drained and rinsed (425g can, 240g drained weight)
- 1 cup cherry tomatoes, halved (about 150g)
- 1/2 cup red onion, finely chopped (about 75g)
- 1/4 cup fresh cilantro, chopped (4g)
- 2 tbsp lime juice (30ml)
- 2 tbsp olive oil (30ml)
- Salt and pepper to taste
- 4 boneless, skinless chicken breasts, grilled and sliced (150-200geach)

Instructions:

1. In a large bowl, combine cooked quinoa, black beans, cherry tomatoes, red onion, and cilantro.
2. In a small bowl, whisk together lime juice, olive oil, salt, and pepper. Pour the dressing over the quinoa mixture and toss to combine.
3. Grill the chicken breasts over medium heat for 5-7 minutes per side or until fully cooked. Let the chicken rest for a few minutes before slicing.
4. Serve the quinoa and black bean salad topped with sliced grilled chicken.

Nutritional Information (Per Serving): Calories: 380 | Fat: 15.1g | Carbohydrates: 23.6g | Protein: 60.3g | Fiber: 6.0g | Sugars: 2.3g | Sodium: 136.7mg

Grilled Chicken Salad with Mixed Greens, Tomatoes, and Vinaigrette

Prep: 15 minutes | Cook: 15 minutes | Serves: 4

Ingredients:

- 4 boneless, skinless chicken breasts, grilled and sliced (150-200g each)
- 6 cups mixed salad greens (spinach, arugula, romaine, etc.) (about 150g)
- 1 cup cherry tomatoes, halved (about 150g)
- 1/2 red onion, thinly sliced (about 75g)
- 1/4 cup fresh basil leaves, torn (about 6g)
- 1/4 cup fresh parsley, chopped (about 15g)
- 2 tablespoons olive oil (30ml)
- 2 tablespoons balsamic vinegar (about 30ml)
- Salt and pepper to taste

Instructions:

1. In a large bowl, combine the mixed greens, cherry tomatoes, red onion, basil, and parsley.
2. In a small bowl, whisk together olive oil, balsamic vinegar, salt, and pepper to make the vinaigrette.
3. Toss the salad with half of the vinaigrette and divide it among four plates.
4. Top each salad with grilled and sliced chicken breasts. Drizzle the remaining vinaigrette over the chicken.
5. Serve immediately.

Nutritional Information (Per Serving): Calories: 320 | Fat: 14.1g | Carbohydrates: 6.1g | Protein: 56.1g | Fiber: 1.7g | Sugars: 3.3g | Sodium: 165.8mg

Spinach and Strawberry Salad with Grilled Chicken

Prep: 15 minutes | Cook: 15 minutes | Serves: 4

Ingredients:

- 4 boneless, skinless chicken breasts, grilled and sliced (each breast approximately 150-200g)
- 6 cups fresh spinach leaves, washed and dried (about 180g)
- 2 cups fresh strawberries, hulled and sliced (about 300g)
- 1/1/4 cup crumbled feta cheese (optional) (30g)
- 1/4 cup sliced almonds, toasted (about 23g)
- 2 tablespoons balsamic vinaigrette dressing (30ml)
- Salt and pepper to taste
- 1/4 cup red onion, thinly sliced (about 40g)

Instructions:

1. In a large bowl, combine the fresh spinach, sliced strawberries, red onion, and crumbled feta cheese (if using).
2. Drizzle the balsamic vinaigrette dressing over the salad and toss gently to coat.
3. Divide the salad among four plates and top each with grilled and sliced chicken breasts.
4. Sprinkle toasted sliced almonds over the salads.
5. Season with salt and pepper to taste and serve immediately.

Nutritional Information (Per Serving): Calories: 290 |Fat: 11.1g | Carbohydrates: 11.2g | Protein: 58.5g | Fiber: 3.4g | Sugars: 5.9g | Sodium: 251.7mg

Mushroom Chicken with Black Rice and Zucchini

Prep: 15 minutes | Cook: 25 minutes | Serves: 4

Ingredients:

- 4 boneless, skinless chicken breasts (each breast approximately 150-200g)
- 1 cup black rice, cooked according to package instructions (about 190g when uncooked, approximately 370g when cooked)
- 2 cups zucchini, sliced (240g)
- 1 cup mushrooms, sliced (about 70g)
- 2 cloves garlic, minced (6g)
- 2 tablespoons olive oil (30ml)
- Salt and pepper to taste
- Fresh parsley, chopped (for garnish) (amount varies as per preference)

Instructions:

1. Season chicken breasts with salt and pepper. In a skillet, heat 1 tablespoon olive oil over medium heat. Cook chicken breasts until golden brown and cooked through, about 6-7 minutes per side. Remove and set aside.

2. In the same skillet, add another tablespoon of olive oil. Sauté garlic, zucchini, and mushrooms until tender, about 5 minutes.

3. Serve chicken over cooked black rice and top with sautéed zucchini, mushrooms, and garlic. Garnish with chopped fresh parsley.

Nutritional Information (Per Serving): Calories: 350 | Fat: 15.4g | Carbohydrates: 34.4g | Protein: 58.8g | Fiber: 2.7g |Sugars: 1.9g |Sodium: 139.3mg

Tender Chicken with Anchovies, Mushrooms, and Lemon-Nut Sauce

Prep: 20 minutes | Cook: 25 minutes | Serves: 4

Ingredients:

- 4 boneless, skinless chicken breasts (150-200g each)
- 1 cup wild mushrooms, sliced (about 70g)
- 1/2 cup peas (about 73g)
- 1/4 cup anchovies, fried until crispy (about 15g)
- 2 tbsp olive oil (30ml)
- 2 tablespoons lemon juice (about 30ml)
- Zest of 1 lemon (1 tbsp)
- 2 tablespoons mixed nuts, crushed (about 20g)
- Handful of microgreens for garnish
- Salt and pepper to taste

Instructions:

1. Season chicken breasts with salt, pepper, and lemon zest. In a skillet, heat 1 tablespoon olive oil over medium heat. Cook chicken breasts until golden brown and cooked through, about 6-7 minutes per side. Remove and set aside.

2. In the same skillet, add another tablespoon of olive oil. Sauté wild mushrooms and peas until tender, about 4-5 minutes.

3. Arrange chicken on plates, top with sautéed mushrooms, peas, and crispy anchovies. Drizzle with lemon juice and sprinkle crushed nuts over the chicken. Garnish with microgreens.

Nutritional Information (Per Serving): Calories: 320 | Fat: 17.1g | Carbohydrates: 4.8g | Protein: 57.9g | Fiber: 1.8g | Sugars: 1.8g | Sodium: 269.0mg

Rice with Julienne

Prep: 15 minutes | Cook: 30 minutes | Serves: 4

Ingredients:

- 1 lb chicken breast, diced (about 454g)
- 10 oz mushrooms, sliced (about 283g)
- 1 onion, finely chopped (150g for a medium onion)
- 2/3 cup 15% cream (or sour cream) (about 160ml)
- 1 tsp olive oil (about 5ml)
- Salt and pepper to taste
- 2.5 oz hard cheese, grated (about 71g)
- Brown rice and fresh herbs for serving (amount varies as per preference)

Instructions:

1. In a skillet, sauté the chopped onion in olive oil until translucent. Add the sliced mushrooms and cook for a few minutes over medium heat.

2. Add the diced chicken breast to the skillet and cook until browned.

3. Season with salt and pepper to taste, then pour in the cream. Simmer for about 5 minutes over low heat.

4. Transfer the mixture into muffin molds and sprinkle grated cheese on top.

5. Bake in the oven for about 20 minutes at 200°C (390°F).

6. Serve with brown rice and fresh herbs.

Nutritional Information (Per Serving): Calories: 350 | Fat: 19.3g | Carbohydrates: 7.7g | Protein: 43.3g | Fiber: 1.3g | Sugars: 4.7g | Sodium: 215.7mg

Turkey Medallions with Creamy Buckwheat & Spicy Vegetables

Prep: 15 minutes | Cook: 20 minutes | Serves: 4

Ingredients:

- 1 lb turkey medallions (about 454g)
- 1 cup buckwheat, cooked (about 170g when cooked)
- Assorted vegetables (zucchini, bell peppers, carrots), diced (amount varies as per preference)
- 1 tbsp olive oil (15ml)
- Salt, pepper

For the sauce:
- 2 tablespoons low-sodium soy sauce (about 30ml)
- 1 tbsp honey (21g)
- 1 tsp grated ginger (2g)

Instructions:

1. Season the turkey medallions with salt, pepper, and your favorite spices. Cook them in olive oil over medium heat until golden brown on both sides and cooked through, about 3-4 minutes per side.

2. Remove from the pan and set aside.

In the same pan, add the diced vegetables and sauté until tender, about 5-7 minutes.

3. Prepare the sauce by mixing low-sodium soy sauce, honey, and grated ginger in a bowl.

4. In a separate pot, cook the buckwheat according to the package instructions.

5. Serve the turkey medallions on a bed of creamy buckwheat mixed with sautéed vegetables. Drizzle the spicy sauce over the top.

Nutritional Information (Per Serving): Calories: 300 | Fat: 5.0g | Carbohydrates: 13.3g | Protein: 36.0g | Fiber: 1.2g | Sugars: 4.4g | Sodium: 554.8mg

Turkey Cutlet with Poached Egg

Prep: 15 minutes | Cook: 20 minutes | Serves: 2

Ingredients:

- 2 turkey cutlets (125g each)
- 2 eggs
- 1/2 cup sun-dried tomatoes, rehydrated and sliced (55g)
- Hollandaise sauce (store-bought or homemade)
- 1 tbsp hemp seeds (10g)
- 1 tbsp chopped walnuts (7g)
- Salt and pepper to taste
- Fresh parsley, chopped
- 1 cup fresh spinach leaves (about 30g)

Instructions:

1. Season turkey cutlets with salt and pepper. In a non-stick skillet, cook the cutlets over medium heat until golden brown and cooked through, about 4-5 minutes per side.

2. While the cutlets are cooking, poach the eggs until the whites are set but the yolks are still runny, about 3 minutes.

3. On each plate, place a cooked turkey cutlet. Top with fresh spinach leaves, poached egg, and sliced sun-dried tomatoes. Drizzle with Hollandaise sauce.

4. Sprinkle hemp seeds and chopped walnuts over the top. Garnish with fresh parsley.

Nutritional Information (Per Serving): Calories: 350 | Fat: 20.8g | Carbohydrates: 18.0g | Protein: 51.3g | Fiber: 4.1g | Sugars: 11.3g | Sodium: 839.2mg

Whole Wheat Turkey-Avocado Wrap

Prep: 10 minutes | Cook: 5 minutes | Serves: 2

Ingredients:

- 2 whole wheat tortillas
- 1 avocado, sliced (200g)
- 1 cup mixed greens (spinach, kale, arugula, etc.) (30g)
- 1/2 red onion, thinly sliced (about 75g)
- 1 tbsp low-fat Greek yogurt (for dressing) (15g)
- Salt and pepper to taste
- 1/2 lb turkey breast, thinly sliced (about 227g)

Instructions:

1. Warm the whole wheat tortillas in a dry skillet over medium heat for about 30 sec. on each side.
2. Lay the warm tortillas flat and layer with turkey breast slices, avocado slices, mixed greens, and red onion slices.
3. Season with salt and pepper. If desired, drizzle with a bit of low-fat Greek yogurt for extra creaminess.
4. Roll the tortillas tightly into wraps. Slice diagonally before serving.

Nutritional Information (Per Serving): Calories: 380 | Fat: 21.1g | Carbohydrates: 36.8g | Protein: 40.1g | Fiber: 11.5g | Sugars: 4.1g | Sodium: 372.1mg

Lavash Rolls with Meat, Vegetables

Prep: 15 minutes | Cook: 10 minutes | Serves: 4

Ingredients:

- 2 large lavash bread sheets
- 1/2 lb lean ground meat (chicken, turkey, or beef) (about 227g)
- 1 bell pepper, thinly sliced (about 150g)
- 1 onion, thinly sliced (150g)
- Salt and pepper to taste
- 1 teaspoon olive oil (5ml)
- 1/2 cup shredded Gouda cheese (about 56g)
- Fresh parsley, chopped (for garnish)
- 1 zucchini, julienned (200g)

Instructions:

1. In a skillet, heat olive oil over medium heat. Add ground meat and cook until browned. Add bell pepper, onion, and zucchini. Cook until vegetables are tender. Season with salt and pepper.
2. Lay out the lavash bread sheets. Spread the cooked meat and vegetable mixture evenly over the lavash.
3. Sprinkle shredded Gouda cheese over the mixture. Roll up the lavash sheets tightly.
4. Slice the rolls into smaller pieces. Garnish with fresh parsley before serving.

Nutritional Information (Per Serving): Calories: 320 | Fat: 14g | Carbohydrates: 28g | Protein: 22g | Fiber: 4g

Plov

Prep: 15 minutes | Cook: 25 minutes | Serves: 4

Ingredients:

- 1 cup basmati rice, rinsed and drained (180-200g)
- 1/2 pound lean lamb or chicken, cut into small pieces (about 227g)
- 1 onion, finely chopped (150g)
- 2 carrots, cut into strips (about 150g total)
- 1 teaspoon ground coriander
- 1/2 teaspoon ground turmeric
- Salt and pepper for taste
- 2 cups low-sodium vegetable or chicken broth (480ml)
- Fresh cilantro, chopped (for garnish)
- 1 teaspoon ground cumin

Instructions:

1. In a large skillet, heat a little olive oil over medium heat. Add meat and cook until golden brown. Remove the meat and set it aside.
2. Add chopped onion to the same pan and fry until translucent. Add the julienned carrots and cook until they are soft.
3. Return the cooked meat to the pan. Add cumin powder, coriander powder, turmeric powder, salt and pepper. Stir.
4. Add the rinsed rice to the pan and stir well to coat the rice with the spice and meat mixture.
5. Pour in vegetable or chicken broth. Cover and place the skillet in the oven until the rice is cooked and the liquid is absorbed, about 20 to 25 minutes.
6. Garnish with fresh chopped cilantro.

Nutritional Information (Per Serving): Calories: 380 | Fat: 2.7g | Carbohydrates: 22.5g | Protein: 19.0g | Fiber: 1.9g | Sugars: 3.9g | Sodium: 140.2mg

Meat with Pumpkin in the Oven and Rice Side

Prep: 15 minutes | Cook: 40 minutes | Serves: 4

Ingredients:

- 1 lb lean meat (chicken, turkey, or beef), cut into cubes (about 454g)
- 2 cups pumpkin, peeled and cubed (about 300g)
- 1 onion, chopped (150g)
- 2 cloves garlic, minced (6g)
- 1 teaspoon paprika
- 1 teaspoon ground cumin
- Salt and pepper to taste
- 2 tablespoons olive oil (30ml)
- 1 cup brown rice, cooked (for serving) (195g when cooked)
- Fresh parsley, chopped

Instructions:

1. Preheat the oven to 375°F (190°C).

2. In a bowl, combine the meat, pumpkin cubes, chopped onion, minced garlic, paprika, ground cumin, salt, pepper, and olive oil. Mix well to coat the ingredients evenly.

3. Transfer the mixture to a baking dish and spread it out evenly.

4. Bake in the preheated oven for 35-40 minutes or until the meat is cooked through and the pumpkin is tender.

5. Serve the meat and pumpkin mixture over cooked brown rice. Garnish with fresh chopped parsley before serving.

Nutritional Information (Per Serving): Calories: 380 | Fat: 12.0g | Carbohydrates: 21.4g | Protein: 32.0g | Fiber: 1.9g | Sugars: 3.7g | Sodium: 61.8mg

Lentil and Vegetable Stew with Tofu

Prep: 15 minutes | Cook: 40 minutes | Serves: 4

Ingredients:

- 1 cup brown lentils, rinsed and drained (about 200g)
- 1 block firm tofu, pressed and cubed (typically around 400g for a standard block)
- 1 onion, chopped (150g)
- 2 carrots, diced (130g total)
- 1 teaspoon ground turmeric
- 3 cups low-sodium vegetable broth (about 720ml)
- 1 teaspoon ground cumin
- Salt and pepper to taste
- 2 tablespoons olive oil (30ml)
- Fresh cilantro, chopped
- 2 celery stalks, diced (about 80g total)

Instructions:

1. In a large pot, heat olive oil over medium heat. Add chopped onion, diced carrots, and diced celery. Cook until vegetables are slightly softened.

2. Add rinsed lentils, vegetable broth, ground turmeric, ground cumin, salt, and pepper. Stir to combine. Bring the mixture to a boil.

3. Reduce the heat to low and let the stew simmer for about 20 minutes or until the lentils are tender and the stew has thickened.

4. In a separate non-stick pan, sauté cubed tofu until golden and crispy.

5. Serve the lentil and vegetable stew in bowls, topped with crispy tofu cubes. Garnish with fresh chopped cilantro before serving.

Nutritional Information (Per Serving): Calories: 320 | Fat: 17.3g | Carbohydrates: 20.7g | Protein: 24.2g | Fiber: 6.9g |Sugars: 5.4g |Sodium: 174.1mg

Meatballs in Tomato Sauce

Prep: 20 minutes | Cook: 25 minutes | Serves: 4

Ingredients:

- 1 pound lean ground meat (beef, turkey, or chicken) (about 454g)
- 1/2 cup brown rice (about 95g when uncooked)
- 1 small onion, finely chopped (about 70g)
- 2 cloves garlic, minced
- 1 teaspoon paprika
- Salt and pepper to taste
- 2 tbsp tomato sauce (30ml)
- 1 cup cherry tomatoes, halved (about 150g)
- Fresh parsley, chopped
- 1 teaspoon ground cumin

Instructions:

1. In a bowl, mix ground meat, brown rice, chopped onion, minced garlic, ground cumin, paprika, salt, and pepper until well combined. Form the mixture into medium-sized meatballs and place them in a baking dish.

2. Add halved cherry tomatoes, tomato sauce, and enough boiling water to cover the meatballs. Bake in a preheated oven at 220 degrees Celsius for 35 minutes. Let the meatballs rest in the turned-off oven for an additional 30 minutes.

3. Garnish with chopped fresh parsley before serving.

Nutritional Information (Per Serving): Calories: 280 | Fat: 4.3g | Carbohydrates: 10.2g | Protein: 30.8g | Fiber: 1.3g | Sugars: 2.0g | Sodium: 81.9m

Meat and Crouton Salad

Prep: 15 minutes | Cook: 10 minutes | Serves: 2

Ingredients:

- 1-2 tbsp Olive oil (15-30ml)
- 1.3 cups diced chicken breast (300g)
- Salt, mixed peppers, paprika (to taste)
- 1 cup Whole grain croutons (60g)
- 1/4 cup Parmesan cheese (20g)
- 4 cups Salad greens: iceberg lettuce, cherry tomatoes (150g lettuce; 150g tomatoes)

For the Dressing:
- 2/3 cup Greek yogurt (150g)
- 1 tsp mustard (5g)
- 2-3 tbsp lemon juice (45ml)
- 1 clove minced garlic (5g)
- Salt, black pepper (to taste)

Instructions:

1. Heat olive oil in a pan over medium heat. Season diced chicken breast with salt, mixed peppers, and paprika. Cook the chicken until fully cooked and golden brown.
2. In a large bowl, combine cooked chicken, whole grain croutons, and salad greens.
3. For the dressing, whisk together Greek yogurt, mustard, Parmesan cheese, lemon juice, minced garlic, salt, and black pepper in a small bowl.
4. Drizzle the dressing over the salad and toss gently to combine.
5. Serve immediately.

Nutritional Information (Per Serving): Calories: 380 | Fat: 16g | Carbohydrates: 18g | Protein: 38g | Fiber: 3g | Sugar: 2g | Sodium: 450mg

Quiche Lorraine

Prep: 15 minutes | Cook: 45 minutes | Serves: 6

Ingredients:

- 1 pre-made pie crust
- 1 small onion, finely chopped (about 70g)
- 150g Gruyère cheese, grated
- 4 eggs
- 300ml heavy cream
- Salt, black pepper, nutmeg (amount varies as per taste)
- 200g bacon, diced

Instructions:

1. Preheat the oven to 180°C (350°F).
2. Line a pie dish with the pre-made pie crust.
3. In a pan, cook diced bacon until crispy. Add chopped onion and cook until translucent.
4. Spread the bacon and onion mixture over the pie crust. Sprinkle grated Gruyère cheese on top.
5. In a bowl, whisk together eggs, heavy cream, salt, black pepper, and a pinch of nutmeg. Pour this mixture over the bacon, onion, and cheese.
6. Bake in the preheated oven for 45 minutes or until the quiche is set and golden brown.
7. Let it cool slightly before slicing and serving.

Nutritional Information (Per Serving): Calories: 420 | Fat: 34g | Carbohydrates: 15g | Protein: 21g | Fiber: 1g | Sugar: 2g | Sodium: 580mg

Green Risotto with Seafood

Prep: 15 minutes | Cook: 30 minutes | Serves: 4

Ingredients:

- 2 1/3 cups Arborio rice (300g)
- 4 1/4 cups vegetable or chicken broth, kept warm (about 1000ml)
- 1 cup green peas, fresh or frozen (145g)
- 2 cups spinach, chopped (200g)
- 2 cups calamari, sliced (200g)
- 2 cups shrimp, peeled and deveined (200g)
- 1 small zucchini, thinly sliced and marinated in lemon juice (200g)
- Olive oil (2 tbsp, 30ml)
- Salt, black pepper (to taste)
- 1/4 cup Grated Parmesan cheese (25g)

Instructions:

1. In a large pan, heat olive oil over medium heat. Add Arborio rice and cook, stirring constantly, until translucent around the edges.
2. Add warm broth, one ladle at a time, stirring frequently and allowing the liquid to absorb before adding more.
3. When the rice is halfway cooked, add green peas and chopped spinach.
4. In another pan, heat olive oil and sauté calamari and shrimp until cooked. Add them to the rice.

5. Add marinated zucchini slices to the rice and stir well. Cook until the rice is creamy and cooked to your desired tenderness.

6. Season with salt and black pepper. If desired, sprinkle with grated Parmesan cheese before serving.

Nutritional Information (Per Serving): Calories: 380 | Fat: 7g | Carbohydrates: 98g | Protein: 32g | Fiber: 6g | Sugar: 4g | Sodium: 920mg

Tuna Salad with Avocado and Crispy Chickpea Popcorn

Prep: 15 minutes | Cook: 10 minutes | Serves: 2

Ingredients:

- 200g tuna steak, thinly sliced
- 1 ripe avocado, diced (200g)
- Mixed greens, cherry tomatoes, corn kernels (amount varies as per preference)
- Ponzu sauce for drizzling
- 1/2 cup chickpea popcorn (50g)
- 2 quail eggs, boiled and halved
- Tahini sauce, Parmesan cheese (amount varies as per preference)

Instructions:

1. In a bowl, combine mixed greens, cherry tomatoes, corn kernels, diced avocado, and chickpea popcorn.

2. Top the salad with sliced tuna and halved quail eggs.

3. Drizzle with tahini sauce and a touch of Ponzu sauce.

4. Garnish with grated Parmesan cheese.

5. Toss gently before serving.

Nutritional Information (Per Serving): Calories: 350 |Fat: 27g | Carbohydrates: 30g | Protein: 33g | Fiber: 11g | Sugar: 4g | Sodium: 570mg

Salmon with Celery Risotto and Wild Rice

Prep: 15 minutes | Cook: 30 minutes | Serves: 2

Ingredients:

- 2 salmon fillets (the weight can vary, typically around 150-200g each)
- 1 cup Arborio rice (200g)
- 1/2 cup wild rice, cooked (about 100g when cooked)
- 1 stalk celery, finely chopped (about 40g)
- 1/2 cup heavy cream (120ml)
- 1/4 cup Parmesan cheese, grated (about 22g)
- 2 tbsp capers, fried (16g)
- Salt, black pepper (to taste)
- Olive oil (amount varies as per preference)

Instructions:

1. Season salmon fillets with salt and black pepper. In a pan, heat olive oil and sear salmon until cooked through.

2. In a separate pan, sauté chopped celery until tender. Add Arborio rice and cook, stirring, until translucent around the edges.

3. Gradually add hot water, one ladle at a time, stirring frequently until the rice is creamy and cooked to your desired tenderness.

4. Stir in cooked wild rice, heavy cream, and grated Parmesan cheese. Cook for a few more minutes until creamy.

5. Serve salmon fillets on top of the celery and wild rice risotto. Garnish with fried capers.

Nutritional Information (Per Serving): Calories: 480 | Fat: 36g | Carbohydrates: 49g | Protein: 36g | Fiber: 3g | Sugar: 1g | Sodium: 580mg

Pasta with Artichokes and Spinach

Prep: 15 minutes | Cook: 10 minutes | Serves: 2

Ingredients:

- 200g whole grain pasta
- 1/2 cup marinated artichoke hearts, sliced (about 90g)
- 1 cup fresh spinach leaves (about 30g)
- 1/4 cup Kalamata olives, pitted and halved (33g)
- 2 tbsp tomato pesto (30g)
- Grated Grana Padano cheese

Instructions:

1. Cook whole grain pasta according to package instructions until al dente. Drain and set aside.
2. In a pan, sauté sliced artichoke hearts, fresh spinach leaves, and halved Kalamata olives until spinach wilts.
3. Add cooked pasta and tomato pesto to the pan. Toss until well combined and heated through.
4. Serve hot, garnished with grated cheese.

Nutritional Information (Per Serving): Calories: 400 | Fat: 10g | Carbohydrates: 70g | Protein: 12g | Fiber: 9g | Sugar: 3g | Sodium: 420mg

Pasta with Mushrooms, Cherry Tomatoes, and Cheese

Prep: 15 minutes | Cook: 15 minutes | Serves: 2

Ingredients:

- 200g whole grain pasta
- 1 cup mushrooms, sliced (about 70g)
- 1 cup cherry tomatoes, halved (about 150g)
- 1/2 cup shredded cheese (such as Parmesan or mozzarella) (about 50g)
- Fresh basil leaves for garnish
- Salt and pepper to taste

Instructions:

1. Cook whole grain pasta according to package instructions until al dente. Drain and set aside.
2. In a pan, sauté sliced mushrooms until golden brown. Add cherry tomatoes and cook until they soften.
3. Add cooked pasta to the pan, toss with mushrooms and cherry tomatoes. Season with salt and pepper.
4. Sprinkle shredded cheese over the pasta and let it melt slightly.
5. Garnish with fresh basil leaves before serving.

Nutritional Information (Per Serving): Calories: 420 | Fat: 14g | Carbohydrates: 65g | Protein: 18g | Fiber: 10g | Sugar: 5g | Sodium: 410mg

Bean Medley Salad with Pan-Seared Shrimps

Prep: 10 minutes | Cook: 5 minutes | Serves: 2

Ingredients:

- 1 can (15 oz) mixed beans, drained and rinsed (about 425g can, approximately 255g drained weight)
- 200g shrimps, peeled and deveined
- 1 tablespoon olive oil (about 15ml)
- 1 teaspoon cumin powder
- Salt and pepper to taste
- Fresh parsley, chopped (for garnish) (amount varies as per preference)
- Lemon wedges (for serving) (amount varies as per preference)

Instructions:

1. In a bowl, combine mixed beans with a drizzle of olive oil, cumin powder, salt, and pepper.
2. Heat olive oil in a pan over medium-high heat. Add shrimps, season with salt and pepper, and cook until pink and opaque, about 2-3 minutes per side.
3. Serve the pan-seared shrimps over the bean mixture. Garnish with chopped fresh parsley and serve with lemon wedges.

Nutritional Information (Per Serving): Calories: 320 | Fat: 12g | Carbohydrates: 38g | Protein: 32g | Fiber: 11g | Sugar: 1g | Sodium: 750mg

Warm Bowl with Brussels Sprouts, Lentil Mix, and Poached Egg

Prep: 15 minutes | Cook: 10 minutes | Serves: 2

Ingredients:

- 1 cup Brussels sprouts, halved (about 88g)
- 1 cup mixed lentils and freekeh, cooked (200g when cooked)
- 1 avocado, sliced (200g)
- Cherry tomatoes, halved
- 2 poached eggs
- Fresh spinach leaves (30g)
- 2 tbsp tahini sauce mixed with a bit of lemon juice (for dressing) (30ml for tahini sauce)
- Popcorn made from chickpeas, mixed nuts, and microgreens for garnish

Instructions:

1. Steam or sauté Brussels sprouts until tender, about 4-5 minutes.
2. In a bowl, layer cooked Brussels sprouts, mixed lentils, freekeh, avocado slices, cherry tomatoes, and fresh spinach leaves.
3. Top the bowl with poached eggs and drizzle with tahini-lemon dressing.
4. Garnish with popcorn made from chickpeas, mixed nuts, and microgreens.

Nutritional Information (Per Serving): Calories: 420 | Fat: 30g | Carbohydrates: 41g | Protein: 25g | Fiber: 16g | Sugar: 4g | Sodium: 210mg

Grilled Vegetable Bowl with Quinoa

Prep: 15 minutes | Cook: 15 minutes | Serves: 2

Ingredients:

- 1 zucchini, sliced (200g)
- 1 red bell pepper, sliced (150g)
- 1 yellow bell pepper, sliced (150g)
- 1 cup cherry tomatoes (150g)
- Olive oil for grilling
- 1 cup cooked quinoa (185g when cooked)
- Salt, pepper, and your favorite herbs for seasoning (amount varies as per taste)
- Fresh basil leaves (for garnish) (amount varies as per preference)

Instructions:

1. Preheat the grill to medium-high heat.
2. Toss zucchini, red bell pepper, yellow bell pepper, and cherry tomatoes with olive oil, salt, pepper, and your favorite herbs.
3. Grill the vegetables until tender and slightly charred, about 10-12 minutes, turning occasionally.
4. Serve the grilled vegetables over a bed of cooked quinoa. Garnish with fresh basil leaves.

Nutritional Information (Per Serving): Calories: 250 | Fat: 8g | Carbohydrates: 54g | Protein: 10g | Fiber: 9g | Sugar: 8g | Sodium: 15mg

Grilled Vegetable Roll with Hummus

Prep: 20 minutes | Cook: 10 minutes | Serves: 2

Ingredients:

- 2 large zucchinis, thinly sliced lengthwise (approximately 400g)
- 1 eggplant, thinly sliced lengthwise (about 550g)
- 1 red onion, thinly sliced into rings (about 150g)
- 1 cup hummus (240g)
- Fresh parsley, chopped (for garnish) (amount varies as per preference)
- Lemon wedges (for serving) (amount varies as per preference)

Instructions:

1. Preheat the grill to medium-high heat.
2. Grill zucchini, eggplant, and red onion slices until tender, about 3-4 minutes per side.
3. Spread a thin layer of hummus over each grilled vegetable slice and roll them up.
4. Arrange the vegetable rolls on a plate, garnish with fresh parsley, and serve with lemon wedges.

Nutritional Information (Per Serving): Calories: 220 | Fat: 16g | Carbohydrates: 37g | Protein: 11g | Fiber: 12g | Sugar: 10g | Sodium: 510mg

CHAPTER 4: DINNER

Salmon with Pine Nuts

Prep: 10 minutes | Cook: 15 minutes | Serves: 2

Ingredients:

- 2 salmon fillets (150-200g each)
- 1/4 cup pine nuts, toasted (about 34g)
- Lemon wedges and spinach leaves for serving (amount varies as per preference)
- Salt and pepper to taste

Instructions:

1. Season salmon fillets with salt and pepper. In a skillet, cook the salmon over medium heat until cooked through, about 4-5 minutes per side.
2. Sprinkle toasted pine nuts over the salmon fillets.
3. Serve hot with lemon wedges and a side of fresh spinach.

Nutritional Information (Per Serving): Calories: 300 | Fat: 20g | Carbohydrates: 2g | Protein: 38g | Fiber: 1g | Sugar: 0g | Sodium: 60mg

Grilled Salmon with Vegetables

Prep: 15 minutes | Cook: 20 minutes | Serves: 2

Ingredients:

- 2 salmon fillets (the weight can vary, typically around 150-200g each)
- Assorted vegetables (eggplant, zucchini, mushrooms) (amount varies as per preference)
- Fresh herbs (rosemary, thyme) for seasoning (amount varies as per preference)
- Salt and pepper to taste
- Juice and zest of 1 lemon

Instructions:

1. Marinate salmon fillets in lemon juice, lemon zest, and a sprinkle of salt for 10 minutes.
2. Grill salmon over medium heat until cooked through, about 4-5 minutes per side.
3. In the meantime, grill assorted vegetables seasoned with salt, pepper, and fresh herbs.
4. Serve the grilled salmon over the vegetables.

Nutritional Information (Per Serving): Calories: 320 | Fat: 10g | Carbohydrates: 10g | Protein: 40g | Fiber: 3g | Sugar: 4g | Sodium: 70mg

Cucumber Rolls with Salmon

Prep: 20 minutes | Cook: 0 minutes | Serves: 2

Ingredients:

- 2 large cucumbers, thinly sliced lengthwise (each cucumber (300g)
- 1/2 cup Philadelphia cream cheese (about 120g)
- 1 ripe avocado, sliced (about 200g)
- Mixed salad greens (amount varies as per preference)
- Sesame seeds for garnish
- Soy sauce for dipping (amount varies as per preference)
- 150g thinly sliced smoked salmon

Instructions:

1. Arrange cucumber slices on a paper towel to absorb excess moisture.
2. Spread a thin layer of cream cheese on each cucumber slice.
3. Place a slice of smoked salmon, avocado, and a few salad greens on top.
4. Roll up tightly and secure with toothpicks. Slice into bite-sized rolls.
5. Sprinkle sesame seeds on top. Serve with soy sauce for dipping.

Nutritional Information (Per Serving): Calories: 250 | Fat: 15g | Carbohydrates: 12g | Protein: 18g | Fiber: 5g | Sugar: 3g | Sodium: 450mg

Baked Fish with Quinoa and Vegetables

Prep: 15 minutes | Cook: 25 minutes | Serves: 2

Ingredients:

- 2 fish fillets (such as salmon or tilapia) (each 150-200g)
- Assorted vegetables (zucchini, bell peppers, cherry tomatoes), diced (amount varies as per preference)
- 1 tablespoon olive oil (15ml)
- Fresh herbs (rosemary, thyme) for seasoning (amount varies as per preference)
- Salt and pepper to taste
- 1 cup quinoa, cooked (about 185g when cooked)

Instructions:

1. Preheat oven to 375°F (190°C). Season fish fillets with salt, pepper, and fresh herbs.
2. In a baking dish, arrange fish fillets and surround them with diced vegetables.
3. Drizzle olive oil over the fish and vegetables. Bake for 20-25 minutes or until fish flakes easily with a fork.
4. Serve the baked fish on a bed of cooked quinoa and roasted vegetables.

Nutritional Information (Per Serving): Calories: 380 | Fat: 12g | Carbohydrates: 44g | Protein: 30g | Fiber: 6g | Sugar: 5g | Sodium: 300mg

Pan-Fried Trout with Almond-Wine Sauce, Peas, and Quinoa

Prep: 15 minutes | Cook: 20 minutes | Serves: 2

Ingredients:

- 2 trout fillets (each fillet typically around 150-200g)
- 1/2 cup quinoa, cooked (about 92.5g when cooked)
- Fresh peas, spinach leaves for garnish (amount varies as per preference)
- 1/4 cup white wine (60ml)
- Lemon zest (amount varies as per preference)
- Salt and pepper to taste
- 1/4 cup almonds, chopped (about 30g)

Instructions:

1. Preheat a skillet over medium-high heat and add a small amount of oil.
2. Season trout fillets with salt, pepper, and fresh herbs. Pan-fry the fillets in the skillet until they are cooked through and have a golden crust, about 3-4 minutes per side. Remove them from the skillet and set aside.
3. In the same skillet, add the white wine and lemon zest. Let it simmer for a couple of minutes to reduce slightly.
4. Add the chopped almonds to the skillet and stir for another 2 minutes until they are lightly toasted and the sauce has thickened.
5. Serve the pan-fried trout on a bed of cooked quinoa, garnished with fresh peas and spinach leaves. Drizzle the almond-wine sauce over the fish and quinoa.

Nutritional Information (Per Serving): Calories: 380 | Fat: 15g | Carbohydrates: 25g | Protein: 25g | Fiber: 4g | Sugar: 2g | Sodium: 350mg

Pan-Seared Tuna with Mango-Avocado Salsa

Prep: 10 minutes | Cook: 5 minutes | Serves: 2

Ingredients:

- 2 tuna steaks (each steak typically around 150-200g)
- 1 ripe mango, diced (200g)
- 1 avocado, diced (about 200g when whole, unpeeled)
- 1/2 cup cherry tomatoes, halved (about 75g)
- 1/4 cup red onion, finely chopped (about 40g)
- Fresh cilantro, chopped (amount varies as per preference)
- Juice of 1 lemon (45ml)
- Salt and pepper to taste

Instructions:

1. Season tuna steaks with salt and pepper. Sear in a hot pan for 2-3 minutes per side for medium-rare.

2. In a bowl, combine diced mango, avocado, cherry tomatoes, red onion, cilantro, and lemon juice.

3. Serve seared tuna topped with mango-avocado salsa.

Nutritional Information (Per Serving): Calories: 300 | Fat: 15g | Carbohydrates: 36g | Protein: 28g | Fiber: 10g | Sugar: 20g | Sodium: 350mg

Tuna Salad with Avocado and Walnuts

Prep: 10 minutes | Serves: 2

Ingredients:

- Mixed salad greens (amount varies as per preference)
- 1 can tuna, drained and flaked (standard can size is about 142g drained weight)
- 1 avocado, diced (about 200g when whole, unpeeled)
- Handful of walnuts (30g)
- Olive oil and lemon juice for dressing

Instructions:

1. In a bowl, combine mixed salad greens, tuna, diced avocado, and walnuts.

2. Drizzle with olive oil and freshly squeezed lemon juice as dressing.

3. Toss gently to combine.

Nutritional Information (Per Serving): Calories: 300 | Fat: 35g | Carbohydrates: 16g | Protein: 26g | Fiber: 9g | Sugar: 3g | Sodium: 380mg

Baked Fish Tacos with Whole Grain Tortillas, Cabbage, and Avocado Salad

Prep: 15 minutes | Cook: 20 minutes | Serves: 2

Ingredients:

- 2 fish fillets (such as cod or tilapia) (each fillet typically around 150-200g)
- 4 whole grain tortillas
- 1 cup shredded cabbage (about 70g)
- 1 avocado, sliced (about 200g when whole, unpeeled)
- Fresh cilantro for garnish
- Lime wedges for serving

Instructions:

1. Season fish fillets with your favorite spices. Bake in the oven until cooked through and flaky.

2. Warm the whole grain tortillas.

3. Assemble tacos: place baked fish on warm tortillas, top with shredded cabbage, avocado slices, and fresh cilantro.

4. Serve with lime wedges.

Nutritional Information (Per Serving): Calories: 350 | Fat: 18g | Carbohydrates: 52g | Protein: 32g | Fiber: 15g | Sugar: 3g | Sodium: 440mg

Seafood Medley Delight

Prep: 15 minutes | Cook: 20 minutes | Serves: 4

Ingredients:

- 1 lb mussels, cleaned and debearded (about 454g)
- 1 lb shrimp, peeled and deveined (about 454g)
- 1/2 lb squid (calamari), cleaned and sliced into rings (about 227g)
- 2 tbsp olive oil (about 30ml)
- 4 cloves garlic, minced
- 1/2 tsp red pepper flakes (optional, for a bit of heat)
- Salt and black pepper
- 1/4 cup fresh parsley, chopped (about 15g)
- 1 lemon, zested and juiced (juice about 45ml)
- 2 cups cooked brown rice (for serving) (about 370g)

Instructions:

1. In a large skillet, heat olive oil over medium heat. Add minced garlic and red pepper flakes (if using). Sauté until fragrant.

2. Add mussels to the skillet and cover. Cook for 5 minutes or until the mussels open. Remove any unopened mussels. Add shrimp and squid rings to the skillet. Cook until the shrimp turn pink and the squid is cooked through, about 3-4 minutes.

3. Season the seafood with salt and black pepper to taste. Add fresh parsley, lemon zest, and lemon juice. Toss everything together to combine.

4. Divide the seafood mixture among plates and serve over cooked brown rice.

Nutritional Information (Per Serving): Calories: 350 | Fat: 8g | Carbohydrates: 51g | Protein: 35g | Fiber: 4g | Sugar: 1g | Sodium: 600mg

Shrimp in Garlic Sauce with Vegetables

Prep: 15 minutes | Cook: 10 minutes | Serves: 2

Ingredients:

- 1 lb mussels, cleaned and debearded (about 454g)
- 1 lb shrimp, peeled and deveined (about 454g)
- 1/2 lb squid (calamari), cleaned and sliced into rings (about 227g)
- 2 tbsp olive oil (30ml)
- 4 cloves garlic, minced (about 12g)
- 1/2 teaspoon red pepper flakes (optional, for a bit of heat)
- Salt and black pepper
- 1/4 cup fresh parsley, chopped (about 15g)
- 1 lemon, zested and juiced (juice about 45ml)
- 2 cups cooked brown rice (for serving) (370g when cooked)

Instructions:

1. In a pan, heat olive oil over medium heat. Add minced garlic and red pepper flakes (if using). Sauté until fragrant.

2. Add peeled and deveined shrimp to the pan. Cook until they turn pink and opaque. Remove the shrimp from the pan and set them aside.

3. In the same pan, add your choice of sliced vegetables (such as bell peppers, broccoli, or snap peas). Stir-fry the vegetables until they are tender-crisp.

4. Season the shrimp and vegetables with salt and black pepper to taste.

5. Return the cooked shrimp to the pan with the vegetables and toss everything together to combine.

6. Garnish with fresh chopped parsley and lemon zest.

7. Serve over cooked brown rice.

Nutritional Information (Per Serving): Calories: 400 | Fat: 10g | Carbohydrates: 45g | Protein: 30g | Fiber: 5g | Sugar: 2g | Sodium: 500mg

Chicken Rolls with Spinach, Feta

Prep: 20 minutes | Cook: 25 minutes | Serves: 2

Ingredients:

- 2 boneless, skinless chicken breasts (each 150-200g)
- 1 cup fresh spinach leaves (about 30g)
- 1/2 cup crumbled feta cheese (about 75g)
- 1 teaspoon olive oil (5ml)
- Salt, pepper, and your favorite herbs/spices to taste
- Toothpicks (amount varies as per need)

Instructions:

1. Preheat the oven to 375°F (190°C).

2. Flatten the chicken breasts using a meat mallet. Season with salt, pepper, and your favorite herbs/spices.

3. Layer spinach leaves and crumbled feta cheese on each chicken breast.

4. Roll up the chicken breasts and secure with toothpicks.

5. Heat olive oil in an oven-safe skillet over medium heat. Brown the chicken rolls on all sides.

6. Transfer the skillet to the oven and bake for 20-25 minutes or until the chicken is cooked through.

7. Remove toothpicks before serving.

Nutritional Information (Per Serving): 320 | Fat: 15g | Carbohydrates: 2g | Protein: 45g | Fiber: 1g | Sugar: 1g | Sodium: 570mg

Baked Chicken Breasts Stuffed with Spinach and Creamy Feta

Prep: 15 minutes | Cook: 25 minutes | Serves: 2

Ingredients:

- 2 boneless, skinless chicken breasts (150-200g)
- 1 cup fresh spinach, chopped (about 30g)
- 1/2 cup creamy feta cheese, crumbled (about 75g)
- Salt, pepper, and your favorite herbs/spices to taste
- Olive oil spray

Instructions:

1. Preheat the oven to 375°F (190°C).
2. Cut a pocket into each chicken breast without cutting all the way through.
3. Mix chopped spinach and crumbled feta in a bowl. Stuff the spinach and feta mixture into the pockets of the chicken breasts.
4. Season the outside of the chicken breasts with salt, pepper, and your favorite herbs/spices.
5. Place the stuffed chicken breasts on a baking sheet lined with parchment paper. Lightly spray with olive oil.
6. Bake for 25 minutes or until the chicken is cooked through and no longer pink in the center.

Nutritional Information (Per Serving): Calories: 320 | Fat: 15g | Carbohydrates: 2g | Protein: 45g | Fiber: 1g | Sugar: 1g | Sodium: 620mg

Baked Chicken and Roasted Vegetable Salad

Prep: 15 minutes | Cook: 25 minutes | Serves: 2

Ingredients:

- 2 boneless, skinless chicken breasts, marinated with salt, pepper, and paprika (around 150-200g)
- 1 zucchini, sliced into large chunks (about 200g)
- 1 red bell pepper, sliced into chunks (about 150g)
- 1 cup mushrooms, halved (about 70g)
- 2 tbsp olive oil (about 30ml)
- Salt and pepper to taste
- Mixed salad leaves (amount varies as per preference)
- Cherry tomatoes, sliced (amount varies as per preference)

For the sauce:
- Cream cheese, Greek yogurt, French mustard (mixed until smooth) (amounts vary as per preference)

Instructions:

1. Preheat the oven to 350°F (180°C).
2. Marinate chicken breasts with salt, pepper, and paprika. Set aside.
3. Place zucchini, red bell pepper, and mushrooms on a parchment-lined baking sheet. Drizzle with olive oil, season with salt and pepper, and toss to coat.
4. Add marinated chicken breasts to the baking sheet.
5. Roast in the oven for 25 minutes or until the chicken is cooked through and the vegetables are tender.
6. In a bowl, mix cream cheese, Greek yogurt, and French mustard until smooth to make the sauce.
7. On a plate, arrange mixed salad leaves, sauce, sliced cherry tomatoes, cooked chicken, and roasted vegetables.

Nutritional Information (Per Serving): Calories: 400 | Fat: 20g | Carbohydrates: 20g | Protein: 35g | Fiber: 5g | Sugar: 10g | Sodium: 450mg

Pasta with Avocado-Lemon Sauce

Prep: 10 minutes | Cook: 10 minutes | Serves: 2

Ingredients:

- 8 oz angel hair pasta (about 227g)
- 1 ripe avocado, peeled and pitted (about 200g)
- Juice of 1 lemon (45ml)
- Fresh basil leaves (amount varies as per preference)
- 2 tablespoons olive oil (30ml)
- Salt and pepper to taste

Instructions:

1. Cook the angel hair pasta according to the package instructions. Drain and set aside.
2. In a blender, combine ripe avocado, lemon juice, fresh basil leaves, olive oil, salt, and pepper. Blend until smooth to make the sauce.
3. Toss the cooked pasta with the avocado-lemon sauce until well coated.
4. Serve immediately, garnished with additional basil leaves if desired.

Nutritional Information (Per Serving): Calories: 550 | Fat: 25g | Carbohydrates: 70g | Protein: 10g | Fiber: 7g | Sugar: 3g | Sodium: 10mg

Pasta in Tomato Sauce

Prep: 15 minutes | Cook: 20 minutes | Serves: 2

Ingredients:

- 8 oz spaghetti (about 227g)
- 1 cup cherry tomatoes, halved (about 150g)
- 2 cloves garlic, minced
- 1 sprig rosemary
- Salt and pepper to taste
- 2 tbsp olive oil (about 30ml)
- 2 tablespoons grated Parmesan cheese (15g)
- 1 cup fresh arugula leaves (about 20g)
- Soy sauce for drizzling

Instructions:

1. In a skillet, sauté cherry tomatoes, minced garlic, and rosemary in olive oil until tomatoes are soft. Blend the mixture with 2 tablespoons grated Parmesan cheese in a blender until smooth.
2. Cook spaghetti according to the package instructions. Drain and toss with the tomato sauce.
3. Serve the pasta topped with halved cherry tomatoes, fresh arugula leaves, and a drizzle of soy sauce.

Nutritional Information (Per Serving): Calories: 420 | Fat: 14g | Carbohydrates: 62g | Protein: 12g | Fiber: 4g | Sugar: 3g | Sodium: 320mg

Pasta with Marinated Olives and Artichokes

Prep: 10 minutes | Cook: 12 minutes | Serves: 2

Ingredients:

- 8 oz farfalle pasta (227g)
- 1/2 cup marinated olives, sliced (about 67g)
- 1/2 cup marinated artichoke hearts, chopped (about 85g)
- 1 cup fresh tomatoes, diced (about 180g)
- Fresh basil leaves
- 3 tablespoons low-fat Parmesan cheese, grated (about 15g)

Instructions:

1. Cook farfalle pasta according to the package instructions. Drain and set aside.
2. In a bowl, combine marinated olives, marinated artichoke hearts, fresh tomatoes, and torn basil leaves.
3. Toss the cooked pasta with the olive and artichoke mixture.
4. Sprinkle with 3 tablespoons grated low-fat Parmesan cheese before serving.

Nutritional Information (Per Serving): Calories: 380 | Fat: 8g | Carbohydrates: 64g | Protein: 12g | Fiber: 6g | Sugar: 4g | Sodium: 590mg

Pasta with Grated Zucchini and Cheese in Cream Sauce

Prep: 10 minutes | Cook: 15 minutes | Serves: 2

Ingredients:

- 8 oz pasta of your choice (about 227g)
- 1 medium zucchini, grated (about 200g)
- Fresh parsley, chopped (for garnish)
- 1/2 cup heavy cream (about 120ml)
- Salt and pepper to taste
- 1/2 cup grated cheese (such as Parmesan or low-fat mozzarella) (about 50g)

Instructions:

1. Cook the pasta according to the package instructions. Drain and set aside.
2. In a pan, sauté grated zucchini until tender. Add cooked pasta, grated cheese, and heavy cream. Stir well until the cheese melts and a creamy sauce forms.
3. Season with salt and pepper to taste.
4. Garnish with fresh parsley before serving.

Nutritional Information (Per Serving): Calories: 480 | Fat: 26g | Carbohydrates: 46g | Protein: 16g | Fiber: 3g | Sugar: 2g | Sodium: 310mg

Creamy Broccoli and Tomato Pasta with Feta

Prep: 10 minutes | Cook: 25 minutes | Serves: 4

Ingredients:

- 12 oz whole wheat macaroni, cooked al dente (about 340g)
- 2 cups broccoli florets, steamed (about 184g)
- 1 large block feta cheese (around 200-400g, depending on brand)
- 1/2 cup cherry tomatoes, whole (about 75g)
- 1/4 cup red onion, finely chopped (about 40g)
- 2 cloves garlic, minced (6g)
- 1/2 cup heavy cream (120ml)
- 2 tablespoons olive oil (30ml)
- Salt and pepper to taste

Instructions:

1. Preheat the oven to 350°F (175°C).
2. In a baking dish, arrange steamed broccoli and whole cherry tomatoes. Place the feta block in the center.
3. Sprinkle red onion and minced garlic over the vegetables and feta. Drizzle with olive oil and pour the heavy cream.
4. Season with salt and pepper. Bake for 20-25 minutes or until the feta is soft and creamy.
5. Cook the macaroni according to the package instructions. Drain and add to the baking dish. Gently toss to combine.
6. Serve hot, garnished with fresh basil if desired.

Nutritional Information (Per Serving): Calories: 565 | Fat: 35g | Carbohydrates: 43g | Protein: 22g | Fiber: 6g | Sugar: 4g | Sodium: 617mg

Mushroom, Zucchini, and Pepper Pasta with Creamy Philadelphia Sauce

Prep: 15 minutes | Cook: 20 minutes | Serves: 4

Ingredients:

- 1 cup mushrooms, sliced (about 70g)
- 1 medium zucchini, diced (about 200g)
- 1 red bell pepper, thinly sliced (about 150g)
- Salt and pepper to taste
- 1/2 cup Philadelphia cream cheese (about 120g)
- 3 tbsp olive oil (about 45ml)
- 1/2 cup low-fat shredded cheese (optional) (about 50g)
- 12 oz whole wheat macaroni, cooked al dente (about 340g)

Instructions:

1. Preheat the oven to 350°F (175°C).
2. In a baking dish, place the Philadelphia cream cheese in the center. Surround it with sliced mushrooms, diced zucchini, and red bell pepper slices.
3. Drizzle olive oil over the vegetables. Season with salt and pepper.
4. Bake for 20 minutes or until the vegetables are tender.
5. Cook the macaroni according to the package instructions. Drain and add to the baking dish. Mix well to coat the pasta with the creamy sauce and vegetables.
6. If desired, sprinkle low-fat shredded cheese on top and bake for an additional 5 minutes until melted.
7. Serve hot, garnished with fresh parsley if desired.

Nutritional Information (Per Serving): Calories: 380 | Fat: 18g | Carbohydrates: 45g | Protein: 12g | Fiber: 7g | Sugar: 7g | Sodium: 370mg

Tagliatelle with Lemon and Basil

Prep: 10 minutes | Cook: 10 minutes | Serves: 4

Ingredients:

- 12 oz (340g) tagliatelle pasta
- 1/4 cup (60ml) olive oil
- Zest and juice of 1 lemon (zest amount varies, juice about 45ml)
- Handful of fresh basil leaves, torn
- Grated Grana Padano cheese, for serving (amount varies as per preference)
- Salt and pepper to taste

Instructions:

1. Cook tagliatelle pasta in boiling salted water according to package instructions until al dente. Reserve half a cup of pasta water before draining.
2. In a large skillet, heat olive oil over medium heat. Add lemon juice, lemon zest, and torn basil leaves. Stir well.
3. Add the cooked tagliatelle to the skillet. Toss to coat the pasta with the lemon and basil-infused oil. Add a splash of reserved pasta water to create a silky sauce.
4. Season with salt and pepper to taste.
5. Serve hot, garnished with grated Grana Padano cheese.

Nutritional Information (Per Serving): Calories: 480 | Fat: 20g | Carbohydrates: 62g | Protein: 14g | Fiber: 3g | Sugar: 2g | Sodium: 220mg

Buckwheat with Vegetables and Mushrooms

Prep: 10 minutes | Cook: 20 minutes | Serves: 2

Ingredients:

- 1 cup buckwheat, rinsed and drained (about 170g uncooked)
- 1 onion, finely chopped (150g for a medium onion)
- 1 cup mushrooms, sliced (about 70g)
- 1 red bell pepper, diced (about 150g)
- 2 tablespoons olive oil (30ml)
- Salt and pepper to taste
- Fresh cilantro, chopped (for garnish) (amount varies as per preference)

Instructions:

1. In a saucepan, heat olive oil over medium heat. Add chopped onion and sauté until translucent.
2. Add mushrooms and red bell pepper. Cook until vegetables are tender.
3. Add rinsed buckwheat and 2 cups of water. Bring to a boil, then reduce heat to low, cover, and simmer for 15-20 minutes or until buckwheat is cooked and water is absorbed.
4. Season with salt and pepper to taste.
5. Garnish with fresh cilantro before serving.

Nutritional Information (Per Serving): Calories: 360 | Fat: 11g | Carbohydrates: 57g | Protein: 9g | Fiber: 7g | Sugar: 4g | Sodium: 20mg

Quinoa-Stuffed Sweet Peppers with Mixed Greens

Prep: 15 minutes | Cook: 25 minutes | Serves: 2

Ingredients:

- 4 sweet peppers, halved and seeds removed (approximately 800g)
- 1 cup quinoa, cooked (about 185g)
- 1/2 cup mixed greens (spinach, kale, arugula, 15g)
- 1/4 cup cherry tomatoes, halved (about 37.5g)
- 2 tablespoons olive oil (30ml)
- Salt and pepper to taste
- Fresh parsley, chopped (for garnish)

Instructions:

1. Preheat the oven to 375°F (190°C).
2. In a bowl, mix cooked quinoa, mixed greens, and cherry tomatoes. Season with salt and pepper.
3. Stuff the sweet pepper halves with the quinoa mixture.
4. Place stuffed peppers on a baking sheet, drizzle with olive oil, and bake for 20-25 minutes or until peppers are tender.
5. Garnish with fresh parsley before serving.

Nutritional Information (Per Serving): Calories: 385 | Fat: 15g | Carbohydrates: 53g | Protein: 11g | Fiber: 9g | Sugar: 10g | Sodium: 40mg

Veggie and Cheese-Stuffed Peppers

Prep: 20 minutes | Cook: 30 minutes | Serves: 2

Ingredients:

- 2 bell peppers, halved and seeds removed (each pepper 150-200g)
- 1 zucchini, diced (200g)
- 1 tomato, diced (180g)
- Salt and pepper to taste
- 1/2 lb lean ground beef or turkey (227g)
- 1 tbsp olive oil (15ml)
- Fresh basil, chopped
- 1/2 cup crumbled feta cheese (75g)

Instructions:

1. Preheat the oven to 375°F (190°C).
2. In a pan, heat olive oil over medium heat. Add ground beef or turkey and cook until browned. Drain excess fat.
3. Add diced zucchini and tomato to the pan. Cook until vegetables are tender. Season with salt and pepper.
4. Remove the pan from heat and stir in crumbled feta cheese.
5. Stuff the pepper halves with the veggie and cheese mixture.
6. Place stuffed peppers on a baking sheet and bake for 25-30 minutes or until peppers are tender.
7. Garnish with fresh basil before serving.

Nutritional Information (Per Serving): Calories: 385 | Fat: 20g | Carbohydrates: 20g | Protein: 30g | Fiber: 5g | Sugar: 10g | Sodium: 350mg

Artichokes with Quinoa

Prep: 15 minutes | Cook: 30 minutes | Serves: 2

Ingredients:

- 2 artichokes, cleaned and halved (300g)
- 1/2 onion, finely chopped (about 75g)
- Olive oil for drizzling
- Handful of fresh herbs (parsley, dill), chopped
- Juice of 1 lemon (45ml)
- 1 cup quinoa, cooked (185g)
- Salt and pepper to taste

Instructions:

1. Preheat the oven to 375°F (190°C).
2. In a bowl, mix cooked quinoa, chopped onion, and fresh herbs. Season with salt and pepper.
3. Fill the halved artichokes with the quinoa mixture.
4. Place artichokes in a baking dish, drizzle with lemon juice and olive oil.
5. Cover with foil and bake for 25-30 minutes or until artichokes are tender.
6. Serve hot, drizzled with any remaining lemon sauce.

Nutritional Information (Per Serving): Calories: 315 | Fat: 6g | Carbohydrates: 55g | Protein: 11g | Fiber: 12g | Sugar: 4g | Sodium: 35mg

Mushroom Ratatouille

Prep: 15 minutes | Cook: 25 minutes | Serves: 2

Ingredients:

- 1 cup mushrooms, sliced (about 70g)
- 1 small eggplant, diced (about 300g)
- 2 tomatoes, diced (240g)
- 2 tbsp olive oil (30ml)
- 1 small zucchini, diced (200g)
- 1/2 red bell pepper, diced (75g)
- 1/2 onion, finely chopped (about 75g for a half onion)
- Salt, pepper, and dried herbs (thyme, oregano) to taste

Instructions:

1. In a pan, heat olive oil over medium heat. Add onions and sauté until translucent.
2. Add mushrooms, eggplant, zucchini, and bell pepper. Cook until vegetables are tender.
3. Stir in diced tomatoes and cook for another 5-7 minutes.
4. Season with salt, pepper, and dried herbs.
5. Serve hot as a side dish or over cooked quinoa for a complete meal.

Nutritional Information (Per Serving): Calories: Fat: 14g | Carbohydrates: 27g | Protein: 5g | Fiber: 8g | Sugar: 13g | Sodium: 25mg

Pan-Fried Tofu with Vegetables

Prep: 15 minutes | Cook: 15 minutes | Serves: 2

Ingredients:

- 1 block firm tofu, pressed and cut into cubes (typically around 400g per block)
- 2 cups mixed vegetables (bell peppers, broccoli, carrots), sliced (300g total)
- 2 tbsp low-sodium soy sauce (30ml)
- 1 tbsp sesame oil (15ml)
- 1 garlic clove, minced (3g)
- 1 tsp fresh ginger, grated(2g)
- Salt and pepper to taste
- Cooked brown rice for serving

Instructions:

1. In a non-stick pan, heat sesame oil over medium-high heat. Add tofu cubes and cook until golden brown on all sides. Remove tofu from the pan and set aside.

2. In the same pan, add garlic and ginger. Sauté for a minute until fragrant.

3. Add mixed vegetables and stir-fry until they are tender but still crisp.

4. Return the tofu to the pan, pour soy sauce over the tofu and vegetables. Toss to combine.

5. Season with salt and pepper to taste. Serve hot over cooked brown rice.

Nutritional Information (Per Serving): Calories: 380 | Fat: 19g | Carbohydrates: 31g | Protein: 29g | Fiber: 6g | Sugar: 6g | Sodium: 540mg

Baked Eggplant with Meat and Vegetables

Prep: 20 minutes | Cook: 25 minutes | Serves: 2

Ingredients:

- 1 large eggplant, sliced into 1 cm thick rounds (weight varies, typically around 550g for a large eggplant)
- 1/2 lb lean ground meat (chicken, turkey, or beef) (approximately 227g)
- 2 tomatoes, sliced (360g)
- 1 cup mushrooms, sliced (approximately 70g)
- 1 bell pepper, thinly sliced (150g)
- 1/2 cup low-fat shredded cheese (about 50g)
- Salt and pepper to taste
- Olive oil for brushing

Instructions:

1. Preheat the oven to 350°F (180°C).

2. Brush eggplant slices with olive oil and season with salt. Place them on a baking sheet lined with parchment paper. Bake for 15 minutes, flipping halfway through.

3. In a skillet, cook ground meat until no longer pink. Drain excess fat if necessary. Season with salt and pepper.

4. On each eggplant round, layer a spoonful of cooked meat, tomato slice, mushroom slices, and bell pepper strips.

5. Sprinkle shredded cheese on top. Bake in the oven for another 10 minutes or until the cheese is melted and bubbly.

6. Serve hot, accompanied by a fresh salad or steamed vegetables.

Nutritional Information (Per Serving): Calories: 370 | Fat: 16g | Carbohydrates: 28g | Protein: 30g | Fiber: 10g | Sugar: 14g | Sodium: 440mg

Baked Eggplant with Tomatoes

Prep: 15 minutes | Cook: 25 minutes | Serves: 4

Ingredients:

- 2 large eggplants, sliced (approximately 550g)
- 4 tomatoes, sliced (approximately 180g)
- Salt and pepper to taste
- 3 cloves garlic, minced (9g)
- Handful of fresh herbs (such as basil or parsley), chopped
- 1/4 cup olive oil (60ml)

Instructions:

1. Preheat the oven to 180°C (350°F).

2. Arrange eggplant slices on a baking tray. Top each slice with a tomato slice, minced garlic, and fresh herbs.

3. Drizzle olive oil over the top and season with salt and pepper.

4. Bake in the preheated oven for 25 minutes or until the eggplant is tender and golden.

5. Garnish with fresh basil leaves before serving.

Nutritional Information (Per Serving): Calories: 190 | Fat: 14g | Carbohydrates: 17g | Protein: 2g | Fiber: 6g | Sugar: 7g | Sodium: 5mg

Baked Zucchini Rolls in Breadcrumbs

Prep: 20 minutes | Cook: 25 minutes | Serves: 4

Ingredients:

- 2 large zucchinis, sliced lengthwise (each 200g)
- 1 cup whole wheat breadcrumbs (about 108g)
- 1/2 cup grated Parmesan cheese (about 50g)
- 1/4 cup (60ml) olive oil
- Salt to taste
- 8 slices Prosciutto (around 30g per slice)
- 8 slices mozzarella cheese (around 28g per slice)

Instructions:

1. Preheat the oven to 180°C (350°F).
2. In a shallow bowl, mix breadcrumbs with grated Parmesan cheese. In another bowl, mix olive oil and a pinch of salt.
3. Dip zucchini slices in olive oil, then coat with the breadcrumb mixture.
4. Lay a slice of Prosciutto and a slice of mozzarella on each zucchini slice. Roll them up and place them seam-side down in a baking dish.
5. Bake for 25 minutes or until the zucchini is tender and the rolls are golden and crispy.

Nutritional Information (Per Serving): Calories: 427 | Fat: 26g | Carbohydrates: 23g | Protein: 24g | Fiber: 3g | Sugar: 3g | Sodium: 1096mg

Mexican Black Bean Salad

Prep: 15 minutes | Cook: 15 minutes | Serves: 4

Ingredients:

- 1 can (15 oz) black beans, drained and rinsed (about 425g can, approximately 255g drained weight)
- 1 cup corn kernels (fresh or frozen) (about 165g if fresh, 155g if frozen)
- 2 tomatoes, diced (240g)
- 1/2 red onion, finely chopped (about 75g)
- 11/4 cup fresh cilantro, chopped (about 4g)
- Juice of 1 lemon (45ml)
- Salt and pepper to taste
- Guacamole for serving

Instructions:

1. In a large bowl, combine black beans, corn, tomatoes, red onion, and cilantro.
2. Squeeze lemon juice over the mixture and toss to combine. Season with salt and pepper.
3. Serve the salad with a side of guacamole.

Nutritional Information (Per Serving): Calories: 194 | Fat: 1g | Carbohydrates: 41g | Protein: 10g | Fiber: 11g | Sugar: 4g | Sodium: 11mg

Greek Salad

Prep: 10 minutes | Cook: 10 minutes | Serves: 4

Ingredients:

- 1 can (15 oz) black beans, drained and rinsed (about 425g can, approximately 255g drained weight)
- 1 cup corn kernels (fresh or frozen) (about 165g if fresh, 155g if frozen)
- 2 tomatoes, diced (240g)
- 1/2 red onion, finely chopped (about 75g)
- 11/4 cup fresh cilantro, chopped (about 4g)
- Juice of 1 lemon (45ml)
- Salt and pepper to taste
- Guacamole for serving

Instructions:

1. In a large bowl, combine salad greens, cherry tomatoes, cucumber, red onion, olives, Feta cheese, and basil.
2. In a small bowl, whisk together olive oil, balsamic vinegar, salt, and pepper.
3. Drizzle the dressing over the salad and toss gently to combine.

Nutritional Information (Per Serving): Calories: 142 | Fat: 10g | Carbohydrates: 11g | Protein: 4g | Fiber: 2g | Sugar: 5g | Sodium: 308mg

CHAPTER 5: DESSERT

Orange Sorbet

Prep: 5 minutes + freezing | Cook: 0 minutes | Serves: 2

Ingredients:

- 2 cups fresh orange juice, strained (about 480ml)
- 1 tbsp honey or a natural sweetener (21g for honey)
- Zest of 1 orange (1 tbsp)
- Fresh mint leaves for garnish (amount varies as per preference)

Instructions:

1. Pour fresh orange juice into an ice cube tray and freeze until solid, usually about 4 hours.
2. Once frozen, transfer the orange juice cubes to a blender or food processor.
3. Blend until smooth and creamy, adding honey or sweetener if desired for extra sweetness. If using, add orange zest and blend again to incorporate.
4. Serve immediately as a refreshing dessert, garnished with fresh mint leaves if desired.

Nutritional Information (Per Serving): Calories: 100 | Fat: 0g | Protein: 1g | Carbohydrates: 25g | Sugars: 20g | Fiber: 0g | Sodium: 0mg

Creamy Coconut Mousse with Fresh Fruits, Nuts, and Chocolate Crumble

Prep: 15 minutes | Chill: 2 hours | Cook: 0 minutes | Serves: 2

Ingredients:

- 1/2 cup unsweetened coconut milk (about 120ml)
- 1/2 cup plain Greek yogurt (low-fat or non-fat) (120g)
- 1 tbsp chia seeds (10-15g)
- 1 tbsp mixed nuts (almonds, walnuts, pistachios), chopped (15g)
- 1 tbsp sugar-free chocolate chips or grated dark chocolate (about 15g)
- Fresh mixed berries (strawberries, blueberries, raspberries) for topping
- Fresh mint leaves for garnish
- 1 tbsp unsweetened cocoa powder (about 5g)

Instructions:

1. Whisk together coconut milk, Greek yogurt, chia seeds, and cocoa powder in a bowl. Refrigerate for at least 2 hours until it thickens.
2. Toast chopped mixed nuts in a dry skillet over medium heat until fragrant. Let them cool.
3. Divide the coconut mousse into serving glasses or bowls.
4. Top with fresh mixed berries, toasted nuts, and sugar-free chocolate chips or grated dark chocolate.
5. Garnish with fresh mint leaves if desired.

Nutritional Information (Per Serving): Calories: 280 | Fat: 16g | Protein: 11g | Carbohydrates: 25g | Sugars: 8g | Fiber: 8g | Sodium: 40mg

Fruit Mousse

Prep: 10 minutes + freezing | Cook: 0 minutes | Serves: 2

Ingredients:

- 1 cup fresh fruits (e.g., mango or strawberries), chopped (165g for mango, 150g for strawberries)
- Fresh mint leaves for garnish
- 1 tbsp honey or a natural sweetener (optional) (21g for honey)
- 1/2 cup low-fat yogurt or Greek yogurt (about 120g)

Instructions:

1. Blend fresh fruits and yogurt in a blender until smooth. Add honey if additional sweetness is desired.
2. Pour the mixture into serving cups or molds.
3. Freeze for at least 2 hours or until the mousse is set.
4. Garnish with fresh mint leaves before serving, if desired.

Nutritional Information (Per Serving): Calories: 90 | Fat: 0g | Protein: 4g | Carbohydrates: 21g | Sugars: 18g | Fiber: 1g | Sodium: 30mg

Chocolate Mousse with Raspberry

Prep: 15 minutes + chilling | Cook: 0 minutes | Serves: 4

Ingredients:

- 1 2/3 cups buttermilk (about 395ml)
- 2 teaspoons chicory powder (about 4g)
- 2 tbsp honey or a natural sweetener (30g for honey)
- 10g gelatin powder, dissolved in 1/4 cup cold water (about 60ml for water)
- 1 cup fresh raspberries (125g)
- Fresh mint leaves for garnish
- 2 tbsp unsweetened cocoa powder (about 10g)

Instructions:

1. In a saucepan, combine buttermilk, chicory powder, cocoa powder, and honey. Heat gently, stirring constantly, until well combined and slightly warmed. Remove from heat.
2. Add the dissolved gelatin to the mixture and stir until fully incorporated. Allow the mixture to cool to room temperature.
3. Divide the fresh raspberries among serving glasses or bowls. Pour the chocolate mixture over the raspberries.
4. Refrigerate the mousses for at least 2 hours.
5. Garnish with fresh mint leaves before serving, if desired.

Nutritional Information (Per Serving): Calories: 180 | Fat: 1g | Protein: 6g | Carbohydrates: 40g | Sugars: 33g | Fiber: 3g | Sodium: 110mg

Sugar-Free Apple Mousse

Prep: 15 minutes + chilling | Cook: 0 minutes | Serves: 4

Ingredients:

- 7 oz (200g) unsweetened applesauce
- 1 packet (10g) gelatin powder

Instructions:

1. Mix gelatin powder into the applesauce in a bowl, stirring well.
2. Melt the gelatin and applesauce mixture over low heat, avoiding boiling. Remove from heat.
3. Transfer the mixture to a bowl, cool slightly, and beat gradually until thickened, about 7-10 minutes.
4. Line the bottom of a serving ring with plastic wrap. Pour the mixture into the ring and refrigerate until set.
5. Once set, remove the dessert from the mold and serve.

Nutritional Information (Per Serving): Calories: 50 | Fat: 0g | Protein: 2g | Carbohydrates: 4g | Sugars: 0g | Fiber: 1g | Sodium: 5mg

Avocado and Blueberry Trifle

Prep: 15 minutes | Cook: 0 minutes | Serves: 2

Ingredients:

- 4.2 oz (120g) ripe avocado
- 5.6 oz (160g) coconut milk
- 3.5 oz (100g) blueberries
- 0.7 oz (20g) pecans
- 1 tbsp lemon juice (15ml)
- Greens for garnish (optional)

Instructions:

1. In a blender, combine coconut milk, ripe avocado, and lemon juice. Blend until smooth and airy.
2. In a separate bowl, crush the blueberries with a fork or blend lightly for texture.
3. In small jars or glasses, layer half of the avocado-coconut mixture at the bottom.
4. Add half of the crushed blueberries on top of the avocado layer.
5. Repeat the layers with the remaining avocado mixture and blueberries.
6. Finish the trifle by adding crushed pecans on top.
7. Garnish with greens if desired.
8. Refrigerate for at least 30 minutes before serving.

Nutritional Information (Per Serving): Calories: 312 | Fat: 27g | Protein: 3g | Carbohydrates: 18g | Sugars: 5g | Fiber: 8g | Sodium: 10mg

Berry Parfait

Prep:10 minutes | Cook: 0 minutes | Serves: 2

Ingredients:

- 1 cup mixed fresh berries (strawberries, raspberries, blueberries) (about 144g for strawberries, 123g for raspberries, 148g for blueberries)
- Fresh mint leaves for garnish (optional)
- 1 cup low-fat yogurt or cottage cheese (245g for yogurt, 226g for cottage cheese)
- 1 tablespoon honey or sugar-free sweetener (optional) (21g for honey)

Instructions:

1. Wash and prepare the fresh berries.
2. In serving glasses, layer the mixed berries with low-fat yogurt or cottage cheese.
3. If desired, drizzle each layer with a small amount of honey or add a sugar-free sweetener for extra sweetness.
4. Repeat the layers until the glasses are filled.
5. Garnish with fresh mint leaves if you prefer.
6. Refrigerate for at least 10 minutes before serving to enhance flavors.

Nutritional Information (Per Serving): Calories: 150 | Fat: 2g | Protein: 10g | Carbohydrates: 33g | Sugars: 26g | Fiber: 6g | Sodium: 130mg

Cinnamon and Walnut Biscotti

Prep: 20 minutes | Cook: 40 minutes | Serves:12

Ingredients:

- 2 cups almond flour (224g)
- 1/2 cup honey (96g)
- 1 tsp baking powder (4g)
- 2 tsp cinnamon (5.2g)
- 1 tsp vanilla extract (5ml)
- 1/3 cup chopped walnuts (40g)
- 3 tbsp unsalted butter, melted (43g)
- 2 large eggs

Instructions:

1. Preheat the oven to 325°F (163°C) and line a baking sheet with parchment paper.
2. In a bowl, mix almond flour, erythritol, baking powder, and cinnamon.
3. Stir in walnuts, melted butter, eggs, and vanilla until well combined.
4. Form the dough into a flat log on the baking sheet.
5. Bake for 25 minutes, then remove and let cool for 10 minutes.
6. Cut into 1/2 inch slices and bake for another 15 minutes, flipping halfway, until crisp.
7. Cool on a wire rack before serving.

Nutritional Facts (Per Serving): Calories: 180 | Sugars: 1g | Fat: 15g | Carbohydrates: 6g | Protein: 6g | Fiber: 3g | Sodium: 20mg

Keto Almond Flour Croissants

Prep: 30 minutes | Cook: 20 minutes | Serves: 8

Ingredients:

- 1 3/4 cups almond flour (168g)
- 1/4 cup coconut flour (30g)
- 1/4 cup unsalted butter, cold (57g)
- 2 tbsp honey (24g)
- 1 tsp baking powder (4g)
- 1/4 tsp salt
- 2 large eggs
- 1 tsp apple cider vinegar (5ml)

Instructions:

1. Preheat the oven to 350°F (177°C) and line a baking sheet with parchment paper.
2. In a food processor, combine almond flour, coconut flour, cold butter, erythritol, baking powder, and salt until mixture resembles coarse crumbs.
3. Add eggs and apple cider vinegar, pulsing until dough forms.
4. Roll out the dough and cut into triangles. Roll each triangle from the base to form croissants.
5. Place on the baking sheet and bake for 18-20 minutes or until golden.
6. Let cool before serving.

Nutritional Facts (Per Serving): Calories: 210 | Sugars: 1g | Fat: 18g | Carbohydrates: 8g | Protein: 7g | Fiber: 4g | Sodium: 50mg

Chia Avocado Pudding

Prep: 10 minutes | Chill: 5-7 hours | Cook: 0 minutes | Serves: 3

Ingredients:

- 300g Avocado, peeled and pitted
- 250ml Coconut Milk
- 30g Chia Seeds
- 30g Honey (or any natural sweetener of choice)
- Juice of 1 Lemon (35ml)
- 20g Pistachios, chopped (for garnish)

Instructions:

1. In a blender, combine peeled avocado, lemon juice, honey, and coconut milk. Blend until smooth and creamy.
2. Add chia seeds to the mixture and stir well to combine.
3. Pour the mixture into individual serving bowls or glasses.
4. Cover and refrigerate for 5-7 hours or until the pudding thickens to your desired consistency due to chia seeds absorbing the liquid.
5. Before serving, garnish with chopped pistachios.

Nutritional Information (Per Serving): Calories: 310 | Fat: 26g | Protein: 4g | Carbohydrates: 27g | Sugars: 16g | Fiber: 9g | Sodium: 20mg

Peach Smoothie

Prep: 5 minutes | Cook: 0 minutes | Serves: 2

Ingredients:

- 400g Peaches, peeled and pitted
- 100g Banana, sliced
- 300ml Yogurt
- 0.5 tsp Honey (optional, depending on sweetness preference) (about 2.5g)
- 1 sprig Mint

Instructions:

1. In a blender, combine peeled and sliced peaches, banana, half a teaspoon of honey (if desired), and a small sprig of mint.
2. Blend until smooth and creamy. The consistency should be thick and velvety.
3. In serving glasses, pour equal portions of yogurt.
4. Pour the blended fruit mixture over the yogurt in each glass.
5. Gently mix the layers.
6. Garnish with a mint leaf or a slice of peach.
7. Serve immediately to enjoy the freshness and goodness of this peach smoothie.

Nutritional Information (Per Serving): Calories: 235 | Fat: 3g | Protein: 7g | Carbohydrates: 51g | Sugars: 37g | Fiber: 5g | Sodium: 65mg

Grape Jelly with Whipped Cream

Prep: 15 minutes | Cook: 0 minutes | Serves: 4

Ingredients:

- 400g Seedless Grapes, washed and removed from stems
- 1 cup Red Wine (or Grape Juice for non-alcoholic version) (240ml)
- 1 cup Whipping Cream (240ml)
- Powdered Sugar (optional, for sweetness)
- 20g Gelatin

Instructions:

1. Soak gelatin in 20g of red wine (or grape juice) in a bowl.
2. Divide grapes into molds or glasses.
3. Heat remaining red wine (or grape juice), add soaked gelatin, and stir until dissolved.
4. Pour mixture over grapes, refrigerate for about 1 hour until set.
5. Whip cream until stiff peaks form. Add powdered sugar if desired.
6. Remove jelly from molds, place on plates, and top with whipped cream.

Nutritional Information (Per Serving): Calories: 235 | Fat: 21g | Protein: 3g | Carbohydrates: 31g | Sugars: 22g | Fiber: 1g | Sodium: 25mg

Baked Apples with Oranges

Prep: 15 minutes | Cook: 30-45 minutes | Serves: 3

Ingredients:

- 3 Apples (546g total)
- 1 Orange (131g)
- 1.5 tsp Honey (about 10.5g)
- 0.5 tsp Cinnamon (1.3g)

Instructions:

1. Grate orange zest and cut the flesh into small pieces.
2. Slice off the top of each apple, remove core, and make a hollow in the center.
3. Place apples in a baking dish, fill centers with orange pieces.
4. Sprinkle with cinnamon, add honey, and garnish with orange zest.
5. Cover and bake at 180°C (350°F) for 30-45 minutes until tender.
6. Cool slightly, garnish with mint, nuts, and extra honey if desired.

Nutritional Information (Per Serving): Calories: Fat: 0.5g | Protein: 0.5g | Carbohydrates: 44g | Sugars: 35g | Fiber: 7g | Sodium: 0mg

Banana Chocolate Bites

Prep: 10 minutes | Freeze: 30-50 minutes | Cook: 0 minutes | Serves: 4

Ingredients:

- 150g Banana
- 20g Unsweetened Cocoa Powder
- 50g Coconut Oil
- 0.5 tbsp Peanut Oil (optional) (about 7.5ml)
- 30g Peanuts (optional)

Instructions:

1. Break the banana into chunks. Melt the coconut oil (heat to at least 25°C or 77°F). Combine all ingredients in a blender and blend until smooth.

Alternatively, mash the banana with a fork and mix it with the other ingredients.
2. Pour the mixture into a silicone mold, preferably one with individual compartments.
3. Optionally, add peanuts to the mixture, slightly submerging them. Walnuts work well with the banana flavor.
4. Freeze for 30-50 minutes. Once set, remove from the mold and cut into bite-sized pieces.
5. Store in the freezer. Thaw in the refrigerator before serving.

Nutritional Information (Per Serving): Calories: 190 | Fat: 19g | Protein: 2g | Carbohydrates: 6g | Sugars: 2g | Fiber: 2g | Sodium: 5mg

Banana Apple Cake

Prep: 15 minutes | Cook: 30-35 minutes | Serves: 8

Ingredients:

- 2 Bananas (236g total)
- 1 Apple (182g)
- 4 Eggs
- 150g Oat Flakes
- 1 tsp Baking Powder
- 0.5 tsp Cinnamon
- 1 tsp Butter (for greasing the pan) (about 5g)

Instructions:

1. Blend bananas into a smooth puree, then add eggs and blend until smooth.
2. Grind oat flakes into fine crumbs; mix with baking powder and cinnamon.
3. Combine the dry mixture with the banana-egg mixture; add diced apple and mix.
4. Grease a baking pan and pour the batter. Bake at 180°C (350°F) for 30-35 minutes.
5. Let it cool, then decorate as desired.

Nutritional Information (Per Serving): Calories: 150 | Fat: 5g | Protein: 6g | Carbohydrates: 22g | Sugars: 6g | Fiber: 3g | Sodium: 74mg

Pear Cake with Honey and Almonds

Prep: 20 minutes | Cook: 50 minutes | Serves: 8

Ingredients:

- 4 Pears (712g total)
- 50g Butter
- 200g Almonds
- 3 Eggs
- 100g Honey
- 150g Flour
- 1 Lemon (58g)
- 2 tsp Baking Powder
- 1 tbsp Vanilla Sugar (12.5g)
- 1 tsp Cinnamon
- Pinch of Salt

Instructions:

1. Peel and quarter the pears, removing the cores. Slice half of the pears into wedges; finely chop the other half and cook until soft, then puree.
2. Beat warm butter with honey, vanilla sugar, cinnamon, lemon zest, and egg yolks. Add pear puree and mix.
3. Sift flour with baking powder, add ground almonds, and fold into the batter.
4. Whip egg whites with a pinch of salt until stiff peaks form; gently fold into the batter.
5. Pour the batter into a greased or lined cake pan. Arrange pear wedges on top.
6. Bake at 180°C (350°F) for about 50 minutes or until a skewer comes out clean.

Nutritional Information (Per Serving): Calories: 350 | Fat: 21g | Protein: 9g | Carbohydrates: 44g | Sugars: 24g | Fiber: 5g | Sodium: 170mg

Lemon Tart

Prep: 20 minutes | Cook: 25 minutes | Chill: 2 hours | Serves: 8

Ingredients:

- 1 1/2 cups almond flour (about 144g)
- 1/4 cup coconut oil, melted (about 60ml)
- 1/4 cup maple syrup or sugar-free sweetener (60ml for maple syrup)
- 4 large eggs
- Zest and juice of 3 lemons (juice about 135ml total)
- 1/4 cup honey or sugar-free sweetener (85g for honey)
- 1/4 cup coconut cream (60ml)
- Fresh berries and mint leaves for garnish (optional)

Instructions:

1. Preheat oven to 350°F (175°C). Mix almond flour, melted coconut oil, and maple syrup (or sugar-free sweetener) in a bowl. Press the dough into the tart pan. Bake for 10-12 minutes; cool.
2. Whisk eggs, lemon zest, lemon juice, and honey (or sugar-free sweetener). Heat coconut cream; whisk into the egg mixture slowly.
3. Pour filling into the cooled crust. Bake for 15-18 minutes until set but slightly jiggly. Cool to room temperature, then refrigerate for 2 hours until firm.
4. Garnish with fresh berries and mint leaves, if desired. Slice and serve chilled.

Nutritional Information (Per Serving): Calories: 280 | Fat: 26g | Protein: 8g | Carbohydrates: 18g | Sugars: 12g | Fiber: 3g | Sodium: 60mg

Coconut Flour Brownies

Prep: 15 minutes | Cook: 25 minutes | Serves:12

Ingredients:

- 60g cocoa powder
- 80g unsalted butter
- 6 large eggs
- 80g xylitol (or sugar substitute of choice)
- 60g coconut flour
- 90g sugar-free chocolate, chopped
- 0.5 tsp salt

Instructions:

1. Preheat the oven to 175°C (350°F).
2. Mix melted butter and cocoa powder until smooth. Add eggs, xylitol, and coconut flour. Stir until well combined; fold in chopped sugar-free chocolate.
3. Line a 20x20 cm baking pan with parchment paper. Spread the batter evenly in the pan.
4. Bake for 25 minutes or until a toothpick inserted into the center comes out with moist crumbs. Be cautious not to overbake; the brownies should be moist.
5. Let the brownies cool completely in the pan. Lift the parchment paper to remove, then slice into squares and serve.

Nutritional Information (Per Serving): Calories: 180 | Fat: 11g | Protein: 4g | Carbohydrates: 13g | Sugars: 1g | Fiber: 4g | Sodium: 130mg

Coconut Flour Muffins

Prep: 10 minutes | Cook: 15 minutes | Serves: 5

Ingredients:

- 3 large eggs
- 35g coconut flour
- 1 tbsp honey (about 21g)
- 0.25 tsp salt
- 3 tbsp coconut oil (45ml)
- Optional: coconut flakes for garnish
- 0.25 tsp baking soda, dissolved in 1 tsp lemon juice (5ml for lemon juice)
- 0.5 cup (200ml) cherries, pitted and halved (about 100g)

Instructions:

1. Preheat to 200°C (400°F). Line muffin tin cups with liners or grease with coconut oil.
2. In a bowl, whisk eggs until frothy. Add honey and coconut oil; mix well.
3. In another bowl, sift coconut flour, salt, and baking soda dissolved in lemon juice.
4. Gradually add dry mixture to the egg mixture, stirring until well combined. Fold in halved cherries. Batter will be thick.
5. Spoon batter into muffin cups, filling two-thirds full. Bake for 15 minutes or until toothpick comes out clean.
6. Let cool in the pan briefly, then transfer to a wire rack. Garnish with coconut flakes if desired.

Nutritional Information (Per Serving): Calories: 156 | Fat: 12g | Protein: 4g | Carbohydrates: 15g | Sugars: 9g | Fiber: 4g | Sodium: 280mg

Light Sugar-Free Coffee Cheesecake

Prep: 10 minutes | Cook: 40-45 minutes | Chill: 1 hour | Serves: 4

Ingredients:

- 3200g cottage cheese
- 150g cream cheese
- 1 ripe banana (about 120g when whole, unpeeled)
- 2 eggs
- 1 tsp instant coffee powder (about 2g)
- 30g coconut flakes

Instructions:

1. Preheat to 160°C (325°F). Place silicone molds on a baking sheet.
2. Blend banana pieces with instant coffee powder until smooth.
3. Add cottage cheese and cream cheese; blend until smooth.
4. Incorporate eggs one at a time, mixing well after each addition.
5. Gently fold in coconut flakes with a spatula.
6. Divide mixture among molds. Bake for 40-45 minutes. Place a dish with hot water on the oven's bottom rack to prevent drying.
7. Let sit in the turned-off oven for 30 minutes. Chill in the refrigerator for at least 1 hour.
8. Garnish as desired before serving.

Nutritional Information (Per Serving): Calories: 235 | Fat: 19g | Protein: 24g | Carbohydrates: 18g | Sugars: 8g | Fiber: 2g | Sodium: 540mg

Fruit and Nut Bars with Seeds

Prep: 20 minutes | Chill: 2-3 hours | Cook: 0 minutes | Serves: 12

Ingredients:

- 250g pitted dates
- 250g dried apricots
- 100g sesame seeds
- 150g mixed nuts (almonds, cashews, walnuts)
- 50g sunflower seeds
- Zest of 1 lemon (1 tbsp)
- 50g dried cranberries
- A pinch of cinnamon
- A pinch of ginger

Instructions:

1. Soak dates and apricots if very dry. Blend into a paste.
2. Toast sesame seeds, sunflower seeds, and mixed nuts in a dry pan over medium heat for 5 minutes.
3. Mix seeds and nuts with fruit paste. Add lemon zest, cranberries, cinnamon, and ginger. Combine well.
4. Divide into bars. Roll in sesame seeds. Refrigerate for 2-3 hours until firm.
5. Slice into bars and enjoy as a healthy snack.

Nutritional Information (Per Serving): Calories: 266 | Fat: 10g | Protein: 4g | Carbohydrates: 30g | Sugars: 21g | Fiber: 4g | Sodium: 5mg

Oat Bars with Nuts and Dried Fruits

Prep: 30 minutes | Cook: 30 minutes | Serves:12

Ingredients:

- 1 cup (250 ml) rolled oats
- 100g nuts
- 150g dates
- 50g raisins
- 50g dried cranberries
- 50 ml apple juice
- 1 tbsp honey (21g)
- 1 tbsp sesame seeds (9g)
- 1 tbsp sunflower seeds (8g)
- 1 tsp vegetable oil (5ml)

Instructions:

1. Soak and blend dates with honey into a paste.
2. Chop nuts, drain raisins and cranberries.
3. Bake oats in the oven at 170°C (340°F) for 10 minutes until golden.
4. Combine oats, nuts, raisins, cranberries, sesame seeds, and sunflower seeds in a bowl.
5. Heat date paste with apple juice in a saucepan until thickened.
6. Mix hot date paste with the oat-nut mixture. Press into a tray.
7. Bake at 170°C (340°F) for 30 minutes until golden.
8. Cool, then cut into bars or squares.
9. Store in an airtight container for up to two weeks.

Nutritional Information (Per Serving): Calories: 180 | Fat: 4g | Protein: 3g | Carbohydrates: 30g | Sugars: 18g | Fiber: 3g | Sodium: 5mg

Homemade Fruit and Nut Candies

Prep: 30 minutes | Chill: 1-2 hours | Cook: 0 minutes | Serves: 12

Ingredients:

- 100g almonds
- 120g walnuts
- 120g dried apricots
- 150g prunes
- 30g coconut flakes
- 2 very ripe bananas (236g total)
- Optional Sweeteners (for a sweeter taste): Honey or syrup

Instructions:

1. Rinse and soak apricots and prunes. Drain well.
2. Finely chop almonds and walnuts.
3. Blend bananas, soaked apricots, and prunes until smooth.
4. Add chopped almonds and walnuts. Mix well.
5. Gradually add coconut flakes until a thick, moldable consistency is achieved.
6. Moisten hands and shape mixture into small candies.
5. Roll candies in coconut flakes or drizzle with melted chocolate.
6. Refrigerate candies for 1-2 hours until firm.
7. Enjoy chilled. Store leftovers in the fridge.

Nutritional Information (Per Serving): Calories: 85 | Fat: 10g | Protein: 4g | Carbohydrates: 23g | Sugars: 13g | Fiber: 4g | Sodium: 5mg

Chocolate Banana Bites

Prep: 15 minutes | Chill: 2 hours | Cook: 0 minutes | Serves: 12

Ingredients:

- 5 rice cakes (or any unsalted whole grain crispbreads) (9g per rice cake)
- 1 ripe banana (120g)
- 3 tbsp cocoa powder (15g)
- 4 tbsp cornflakes, unsweetened (15g)
- Optional: Dates (4-6 pieces, soaked if dry, 24-36g) or dried apricots (8g per apricot) for added sweetness

Instructions:

1. Chop banana, crush rice cakes, and chop dates/apricots if using.
2. Blend rice cakes, banana, and dates/apricots into a dough-like consistency.
3. Mix in cocoa powder until dense and playdough-like. Adjust with extra rice cake or cocoa if needed.
4. Crush cornflakes finely, place in a bowl.
5. Wet hands, shape mixture into small balls or cookies. Roll in crushed cornflakes to coat evenly.
6. Refrigerate bites for 2 hours or until firm.
7. Enjoy chilled. Store leftovers in the fridge for up to two days.

Nutritional Information (Per Serving): Calories: 55 | Fat: 0.5g | Protein: 1g | Carbohydrates: 14g | Sugars: 6g | Fiber: 1.5g | Sodium: 0.5mg

Peanut Butter Cups

Prep: 30 minutes | Cook: 0 minutes | Serves: 12

Ingredients:

- 1 1/4 cups oat flour (125g)
- 2 tbsp peanut butter (32g)
- 1/4 cup water (60ml)
- Sweetener to taste
- 1 egg yolk (about 14g)
- 3 tbsp cornstarch (24g)
- 1 pack vanilla extract (2g or 5ml)
- 3 tsp cocoa powder (6g)
- 1 tsp instant coffee (2g)
- Peanuts for garnish
- Dark chocolate (optional)

Instructions:

1. Mix oat flour, peanut butter, water, and sweetener to form dough. Shape into cups and bake at 180°C for 10 minutes. Cool.

2. Prepare chocolate coffee cream with egg yolk, sweetener, cornstarch, milk, cocoa powder, and coffee.
3. Fill cooled cups with warm chocolate coffee cream. Garnish with peanuts.
4. Optionally, drizzle melted dark chocolate on top.
5. Chill before serving.

Nutritional Information (Per Serving): Calories: 120 | Fat: 3g | Protein: 3g | Carbohydrates: 12g | Sugars: 1g | Fiber: 1.5g | Sodium: 20mg

Oat Baskets with Cottage Cheese and Berries

Prep: 15 minutes | Cook: 25 minutes | Serves: 4

Ingredients:

- 1/4 cup rolled oats (30g)
- 2 tbsp almond flour (20g)
- 1 egg yolk (about 14g)
- 1/2 cup cottage cheese (100g)
- Sugar substitute, to taste
- 1/2 tsp agar-agar or pectin (about 1.5g)
- Assorted berries for topping
- 1 tsp honey (about 7g)
- Pinch of salt

Instructions:

1. Separate egg yolk from the egg white.
2. Mix oats, almond flour, egg white, honey, and a pinch of salt in a bowl until a pliable dough forms.
3. Press the mixture into greased tartlet molds and bake at 200°C (390°F) for 10 minutes.
4. Blend cottage cheese with egg yolk and sugar substitute until smooth.
5. Fill baked baskets with the cottage cheese mixture and bake for 10-15 more minutes at 190°C (375°F).
6. Prepare agar-agar gel, pour it over assorted berries on the baskets.

Nutritional Information (Per Serving): Calories: 150 | Fat: 5g | Protein: 8g | Carbohydrates: 14g | Sugars: 2g | Fiber: 2g | Sodium: 175mg

Almond Cookies

Prep: 15 minutes | Cook: 12 minutes | Serves: 20

Ingredients:

- 2 cups almond flour (192g)
- 1/4 cup sugar substitute (like erythritol or stevia)
- 1 tsp vanilla extract (5ml)
- 1/4 teaspoon salt
- 1/4 cup coconut oil, melted (about 60ml)

Instructions:

1. Preheat the oven to 350°F (175°C) and line a baking sheet with parchment paper.
2. In a bowl, combine almond flour, melted coconut oil, sugar substitute, vanilla extract, and salt. Mix until a dough forms.
3. Scoop out tablespoon-sized portions of dough and shape them into cookies. Place them on the prepared baking sheet.
4. Flatten each cookie gently with a fork.
5. Bake for 10-12 minutes or until the edges turn golden brown.
6. Allow the cookies to cool on the baking sheet for 5 minutes before transferring them to a wire rack to cool completely.

Nutritional Information (Per Serving): Calories: 90 | Fat: 7g | Protein: 2g | Carbohydrates: 3g | Sugars: 0g | Fiber: 1g | Sodium: 25mg

Nut and Fruit Roll

Prep: 15 minutes | Cook: 10 minutes | Serves: 8

Ingredients:

- 1/2 cup dried fruits (like apricots, dates, or figs), finely chopped (about 90g)
- 1 whole-grain lavash wrap (around 30-50g)
- 1 cup mixed nuts, finely chopped (about 120g)

Instructions:

1. Mix finely chopped nuts and dried fruits in a bowl.
2. Spread the nut and fruit mixture evenly over the lavash wrap.
3. Roll the lavash tightly around the filling.
4. Refrigerate for 30 minutes to set.
5. Slice into 1-inch thick pieces before serving.

Nutritional Information (Per Serving): Calories: 150 | Fat: 11g | Protein: 5g | Carbohydrates: 19g | Sugars: 10g | Fiber: 4g | Sodium: 10mg

Oat Cookies with Apples, Raisins, and Nuts

Prep: 20 minutes | Cook: 15 minutes | Serves: 24

Ingredients:

- 1 1/2 cups old-fashioned oats (about 135g)
- 1 cup almond flour (96g)
- 1 tsp ground cinnamon
- 1/2 teaspoon baking powder
- 1/4 teaspoon salt
- 1/4 cup coconut oil, melted (about 60ml)
- 1/4 cup raisins (about 40g)
- 1/4 cup unsweetened applesauce (about 60g)
- 1/4 cup sugar substitute (like erythritol or stevia) (amount varies as per specific product)
- 1/2 cup chopped apples (65g)
- 1/4 cup chopped nuts (30g)

Instructions:

1. Preheat the oven to 350°F (175°C) and line a baking sheet with parchment paper.
2. In a bowl, combine oats, almond flour, ground cinnamon, baking powder, and salt.
3. In another bowl, mix melted coconut oil, applesauce, and sugar substitute.
4. Combine the wet and dry ingredients. Fold in chopped apples, raisins, and nuts.
5. Drop tablespoon-sized portions of dough onto the prepared baking sheet, spacing them apart.
6. Flatten each cookie slightly with the back of a spoon.
7. Bake for 12-15 minutes or until the cookies are golden around the edges.
8. Let the cookies cool on the baking sheet for a few minutes before transferring them to a wire rack to cool completely.

Nutritional Information (Per Serving): Calories: 80 | Fat: 5g | Protein: 1g | Carbohydrates: 7g | Sugars: 1g | Fiber: 1g | Sodium: 25mg

Cottage Cheese Banana Ice Cream

Prep: 10 minutes | Freeze: 4 hours | Cook: 0 minutes | Serves: 4

Ingredients:

- 200g low-fat cottage cheese
- 5 tbsp natural yogurt (75g)
- 170g ripe banana, sliced
- 1 ripe peach, peeled, pitted, and diced (150g)
- 1 tbsp honey (about 21g)

Instructions:

1. In a bowl, combine low-fat cottage cheese and natural yogurt. Mix well to remove lumps.
2. Add liquid honey and blend until smooth using a hand blender. If you don't have a blender, strain the cottage cheese and finely grate the banana instead.
3. Add sliced banana and diced peach to the mixture. Stir until well incorporated.
4. Pour the mixture into individual molds or a silicone ice cube tray.
5. Freeze for at least 4 hours or until solid.
6. Serve the cottage cheese banana ice cream chilled.

Nutritional Information (Per Serving): Calories: 120 | Fat: 1g | Protein: 7g | Carbohydrates: 19g | Sugars: 13g | Fiber: 2g | Sodium: 123mg

Cottage Cheese Dessert with Berries

Prep: 10 minutes | Cook: 0 minutes | Serves: 2

Ingredients:

- 1/2 cup mixed berries (strawberries, blueberries, raspberries) (about 74g)
- 1 tbsp honey (21g)
- 1 cup low-fat cottage cheese (226g)

Instructions:

1. In a bowl, combine cottage cheese with mixed berries.
2. Sweeten with honey or stevia if desired.
3. Mix well and refrigerate until serving.
4. Garnish with extra berries before serving.

Nutritional Information (Per Serving): Calories: 150 | Fat: 2g | Protein: 15g | Carbohydrates: 24g | Sugars: 20g | Fiber: 3g | Sodium: 391mg

Cottage Cheese Bake with Raisins

Prep: 15 minutes | Cook: 25 minutes | Serves: 4

Ingredients:

- 2 cups low-fat cottage cheese (about 452g)
- 3 tbsp raisins (about 27g)
- 1 tablespoon honey or stevia (about 21g for honey)
- 1 teaspoon vanilla extract (about 5ml)
- 2 eggs
- 2 tablespoons whole-grain flour (about 16g)

Instructions:

1. Preheat the oven to 350°F (175°C) and grease a baking dish.
2. In a bowl, mix cottage cheese, raisins, honey (or stevia), and vanilla extract.
3. Add eggs and mix well. Gradually stir in the whole-grain flour.
4. Pour the mixture into the prepared baking dish.
5. Bake for 25 minutes or until the top is golden brown.
6. Let it cool slightly before serving.

Nutritional Information (Per Serving): Calories: 180 | Fat: 6g | Protein: 21g | Carbohydrates: 22g | Sugars: 16g | Fiber: 1g | Sodium: 373mg

CHAPTER 6: SALADS

Vegetable Bowl with Quail Eggs

Prep: 15 minutes | Cook: 10 minutes | Serves: 1

Ingredients:

- 1 medium carrot (100g)
- 3 quail eggs
- 1/2 cup cherry tomatoes (80g)
- 1 small cucumber (100g)
- 2 medium celery stalks (60g)
- 1 small sweet bell pepper (80g)
- 1/2 medium avocado (70g)
- 2 cups spinach (50g)
- 1/4 cup green onions (20g)
- 2 tbsp olive oil (30ml)
- 1 tbsp lemon juice (20ml)
- Salt, to taste
- Black pepper, to taste

Instructions:

1. Chop all vegetables as desired. Spinach leaves should be soaked and dried to crispness.
2. Arrange spinach leaves in a deep bowl. Add grated carrots. Place cucumber and celery on top.
3. Include sweet bell peppers and halved cherry tomatoes.
4. Boil quail eggs for 5 minutes, cool, peel, and cut them in half.
5. Add quail eggs and sliced avocado to the bowl.
6. Season with salt, black pepper, and drizzle with olive oil and lemon juice. Serve immediately for the best taste and nutrition.

Nutritional Information (Per Serving): Calories: 230 | Fat: 32g | Protein: 11g | Carbohydrates: 23g | Sugars: 9g | Fiber: 9g | Sodium: 126mg

Beef Tongue Salad with Creamy Dressing

Prep: 15 minutes | Cook: 15 minutes | Serves: 4

Ingredients:

- 100g boiled beef tongue
- 2 eggs
- 1 cucumber (about 300g for a medium cucumber)
- 120g Napa cabbage
- 1 tsp Greek yogurt (5g)
- 2 tsp cream cheese (preferably "Philadelphia") (about 10g)
- Salt, to taste
- Black pepper, to taste
- Green onions, for garnish

Instructions:

1. Wash and finely chop the Napa cabbage. Slice the cucumber into a spiral for decoration.
2. Boil the eggs until done, cool in cold water, peel, and cut into small pieces.
3. Peel the boiled beef tongue. If it's difficult to peel, soak it in cold water; it will make the peeling process easier. Slice the tongue into thin strips.
4. In a small bowl, mix Greek yogurt and cream cheese until smooth. Season with salt and black pepper to taste.
5. In a large bowl, combine the chopped Napa cabbage, boiled eggs, beef tongue slices, and the creamy dressing. Mix well to coat the ingredients evenly.
6. Divide the salad into two plates. Garnish with cucumber spirals and chopped green onions.

Nutritional Information (Per Serving): Calories: 280 | Fat: 12g | Protein: 15g | Carbohydrates: 8g | Sugars: 3g | Fiber: 2g | Sodium: 380mg

Warm Asparagus Salad with Vegetables and Egg

Prep: 15 minutes | Cook: 25 minutes | Serves: 4

Ingredients:

- 200g asparagus
- 2 eggs
- 2 small cucumbers (about 200g each, so 400g total)
- 10 radishes (90g)
- 1 red onion (150g)
- 1 tbsp olive oil (15ml)
- 1 tsp ground coriander
- Salt, to taste
- 2 tsp balsamic vinegar (10ml)
- 1 tbsp sesame seeds (9g)
- Fresh herbs (optional, for garnish)
- Black pepper, to taste

Instructions:

1. Trim the tough ends of the asparagus and peel the thicker stalks if necessary. Cut into bite-sized pieces.
2. Bring a pot of salted water to a boil. Add asparagus and blanch for 2 minutes. Immediately transfer asparagus to a bowl of ice water to cool. Drain and pat dry with a clean kitchen towel.
3. Boil eggs until hard-boiled, approximately 9-10 minutes. Cool in cold water, peel, and cut into quarters.
4. Slice radishes and cucumbers. Thinly slice the red onion.
5. In a pan, heat olive oil over medium heat. Add red onion slices and sauté for 3-4 minutes until translucent. Add coriander, black pepper, radishes, and cucumbers. Sauté for another 3-4 minutes.
6. Add blanched asparagus to the pan. Mix well and cover with a lid. Let it sit for 5 minutes to blend the flavors.
7. Divide the vegetable mixture into plates. Arrange quartered eggs on top. Sprinkle with sesame seeds. Drizzle balsamic vinegar over the salad.
8. Garnish with fresh herbs if desired.

Nutritional Information (Per Serving): Calories: 180 | Fat: 6g | Protein: 7g | Carbohydrates: 18g | Sugars: 8g | Fiber: 5g | Sodium: 85mg

Warm Beef Salad

Prep: 20 minutes | Cook: 25 minutes | Serves: 4

Ingredients:

- 1 cup diced beef (200g)
- 1 carrot, grated (about 61g)
- 1 onion, finely chopped (about 150g)
- 1 handful of mixed greens (lettuce, arugula) (20g)
- 1 bell pepper, diced (150g)
- 2 cucumbers, peeled and sliced (about 600g)
- 7 cherry tomatoes, halved (about 105g)
- 1 tbsp olive oil (15ml)
- 2 tbsp soy sauce (30ml)
- 1 tsp honey (7g)

Instructions:

1. In a small bowl, mix olive oil, soy sauce, and honey to create the dressing.
2. Cook the diced beef in a non-stick pan over medium heat for 40 minutes without adding oil. Add finely chopped onion and grated carrot. Cook for an additional 10 minutes until tender.
3. Slice the bell pepper, chop the mixed greens, peel and slice the cucumbers, and halve the cherry tomatoes.
4. In a large salad bowl, combine diced bell pepper, sliced cucumber, mixed greens, cherry tomatoes, and the cooked beef mixture.
5. Pour the prepared sauce over the salad. Toss everything gently to combine.

Nutritional Information (Per Serving): Calories: 280 | Fat: 14g | Protein: 20g | Carbohydrates: 22g | Sugars: 14g | Fiber: 4g | Sodium: 560mg

Beef and Pickled Cucumber Salad

Prep: 20 minutes | Cook: 1 hour | Serves: 4

Ingredients:

- 1 cup boiled beef, diced (250g)
- 1 cup cooked beans, drained (150g)
- Fresh herbs (dill, parsley, green onion), finely chopped (15g total)
- 1 cup pickled cucumbers, sliced (250g)
- 1/2 cup chopped onion (100g)
- Salt and black pepper
- 1 tbsp lemon or lime juice
- 1 tbsp oil, to taste (15ml)

Instructions:

1. Boil and dice beef. Cook and drain beans. Slice pickled cucumbers. Finely chop onion. Wash and chop fresh herbs.
2. Mix chopped onion with sugar, a pinch of salt, and lemon or lime juice. Let it marinate for 15-20 minutes, then drain.
3. Combine diced beef, cooked beans, pickled cucumbers, marinated onion, and fresh herbs in a bowl.
4. Season with salt and ground black pepper. Drizzle with lemon or lime juice and sunflower oil.
5. Gently toss to combine flavors.
6. Let the salad marinate briefly.

Nutritional Information (Per Serving): Calories: 280 | Fat: 11g | Protein: 17g | Carbohydrates: 16g | Sugars: 3g | Fiber: 6g | Sodium: 790mg

Turkey and Vegetable Salad

Prep: 20 minutes | Cook: 15 minutes | Serves: 4

Ingredients:

- 1 1/2 cups diced turkey fillet (380g)
- 3/4 cup cherry tomatoes, halved (170g)
- 1/2 cup mixed greens (parsley, dill, green onion) (50g)
- 2 tsp lemon juice (10ml)
- 2 tbsp olive oil (30ml)
- 1 tbsp honey (15g)
- 1/4 tsp dry adjika spice (1g)
- 1/4 cup red onion, thinly sliced (50g)
- Salt and black pepper, to taste
- 1 cup diced cucumber (200g)

Instructions:

1. Rinse the mixed greens thoroughly and soak in cold water for 15-20 minutes. Drain excess water and set aside.
2. Heat 10ml of olive oil in a deep skillet. Add diced turkey and cook for 2-3 minutes over high heat, stirring occasionally. Reduce heat, cover, and cook for another 10-15 minutes until turkey is cooked through.
3. Season the cooked turkey with salt and black pepper to taste. Remove from heat and place on a paper towel to remove excess oil.

4. In a small jar, combine 20ml olive oil, lemon juice, honey, and dry adjika spice. Cover the jar with parchment paper under the lid to avoid contact with the metal. Shake well to mix.
5. In a large bowl, combine soaked mixed greens, thinly sliced red onion, diced cucumber, halved cherry tomatoes, and cooked turkey pieces.
6. Drizzle the prepared dressing over the salad. Gently toss to combine all ingredients.
7. Season with additional salt and black pepper if needed. Serve immediately for the freshest taste.

Nutritional Information (Per Serving): Calories: 320 | Fat: 15g | Protein: 30g | Carbohydrates: 17g | Sugars: 10g | Fiber: 2g | Sodium: 360mg

Turkey Salad with Pomegranate and Citrus Dressing

Prep: 20 minutes | Cook: 20 minutes | Serves: 4

Ingredients:

- 1 1/4 cups turkey fillet (300g)
- 2 tbsp olive oil (30ml)
- 1 medium red onion, finely chopped (150g)
- 1/2 cup mandarin juice (120ml)
- 1 tsp honey (7g)
- 2 cups mixed salad greens (200g)
- 2 tbsp pumpkin seeds (20g)
- 1 medium pomegranate, seeds removed (280g)

Instructions:

1. Wash and dry the turkey fillet. Cut into small pieces and season with your choice of spices.
2. Heat olive oil in a skillet and cook the turkey slices in batches until browned and cooked through, about 2-3 minutes. Remove from the skillet.
3. In the same skillet, add the finely chopped red onion and sauté until translucent. Pour in the mandarin juice (about 1/2 cup) and add honey. Stir and cook for 3 minutes until it thickens into a syrupy consistency. You can substitute mandarin juice with orange or grapefruit juice.

4. Arrange mixed salad greens on plates. Top with turkey slices and drizzle with the warm citrus dressing. Sprinkle pumpkin seeds over the salad.

5. Cut the pomegranate into quarters and remove the seeds. Sprinkle the salad with pomegranate seeds and, if desired, a splash of balsamic vinegar before serving.

Nutritional Information (Per Serving): Calories: 320 | Fat: 14g | Protein: 24g | Carbohydrates: 29g | Sugars: 17g | Fiber: 5g | Sodium: 72mg

Turkey Salad with Beans and Sweet Pepper

Prep: 20 minutes | Cook: 20 minutes | Serves: 4

Ingredients:

- 1 1/4 cups boiled turkey, shredded (300g)
- 1 cup canned beans (200g)
- 2 cups sweet bell pepper, julienned (300g)
- 1 cup red onion, thinly sliced (150g)
- 1 clove garlic, minced (3g)
- 1/4 cup fresh herbs (parsley, dill, cilantro), chopped (20g)
- 3 tbsp vegetable oil (45ml)
- 1/4 cup 9% vinegar (60ml)
- 1 tsp mustard (5g)
- 1/2 tsp salt
- 3/4 cup water (for marinade) (200ml)

Instructions:

1. Slice the red onion into half rings. Prepare a marinade by mixing 200ml water with 60ml vinegar. Let the onion marinate in this mixture for 20 minutes.

2. Rinse the sweet bell pepper, remove the core, and julienne it.

3. Finely chop the fresh herbs.

4. Slice the boiled turkey into thin strips.

5. Prepare the dressing for the salad. Mix minced garlic, mustard, and a pinch of salt with vegetable oil.

6. Drain the marinated onion. In a large bowl, combine marinated onion, sweet bell pepper, fresh herbs, boiled turkey, and canned beans.

7. Pour the prepared dressing over the salad and mix well.

8. Let the salad marinate for 15-20 minutes before serving. Adjust salt and acidity to taste if needed.

Nutritional Information (Per Serving): Calories: 250 | Fat: 13g | Protein: 20g | Carbohydrates: 24g | Sugars: 5g | Fiber: 7g | Sodium: 425mg

Christmas Wreath Salad

Prep: 15 minutes | Cook: 10 minutes | Serves: 2

Ingredients:

- 2 3/4 cups broccoli (400g)
- 1 pack cherry tomatoes (around 1 1/2 cups, 250g)
- 1 pack mini mozzarella (about 1 cup, 150g)
- 2 yellow tomatoes (about 2 cups, 360g total)
- 2 garlic cloves (6g total)
- 1/2 cup Greek yogurt (100g)
- Juice of 0.5 lemon (about 1-1.5 tbsp, 15-20ml)
- Spices (your choice)
- Salt, to taste

Instructions:

1. Sauté broccoli in butter, add crushed garlic.

2. Add a bit of water, simmer for 7-10 minutes until desired tenderness. Season with salt and lemon juice.

3. Dry the broccoli on paper towels.

4. Cut a bow shape from one tomato, then chop the rest of the tomatoes.

5. Place a bowl of sauce in the center of the plate, surround it with broccoli and tomatoes.

6. Add mini mozzarella balls and cherry tomatoes. Place the tomato bow on top.

7. For the sauce, mix Greek yogurt, chosen spices, salt, and lemon juice.

8. Drizzle the sauce over the salad.

9. Optionally, garnish with cheese stars and tomato slices.

Nutritional Information (Per Serving): Calories: 180 | Fat: 14g | Protein: 24g | Carbohydrates: 26g | Sugars: 14g | Fiber: 8g | Sodium: 477mg

Cabbage, Corn, and Chicken Salad

Prep: 15 minutes | Cook: 10 minutes | Serves: 2

Ingredients:

- 2 1/2 cups white cabbage, thinly sliced or grated (400g)
- 1 1/2 cups chicken breast, boiled and shredded (200g)
- 1 cup corn kernels, boiled or canned (150g)
- 1 medium apple, thinly sliced (approximately 182g)
- 1 yellow bell pepper, finely chopped (about 150g)
- 1/4 cup green onions, finely chopped (15g)
- 2 tbsp fresh parsley, finely chopped (10g)
- 2 tbsp sunflower oil (30ml)
- 1 tsp grainy mustard (5g)
- 1/2 tsp salt

Instructions:

1. Boil the chicken breast until cooked through. Drain and shred into small pieces.
2. Boil or drain canned corn kernels. Set aside to cool.
3. Thinly slice or grate the cabbage. Place it in a large bowl, add a pinch of salt, and massage the cabbage to soften it.
4. Slice the apple into thin wedges, removing the core. Add the apple slices to the bowl.
5. Finely chop the yellow bell pepper and add it to the bowl along with the boiled chicken and corn.
6. In a small bowl, mix sunflower oil, grainy mustard, and a pinch of salt to create the dressing.
7. Pour the dressing over the salad and toss well to combine.
8. Garnish the salad with chopped green onions and fresh parsley.

Nutritional Information (Per Serving): Calories: 250 | Fat: 21g | Protein: 29g | Carbohydrates: 38g | Sugars: 16g | Fiber: 9g | Sodium: 674mg

Chicken, Rice, and Vegetable Salad

Prep: 20 minutes | Cook: 5 minutes | Serves: 2

Ingredients:

- 1/2 cup carrots, peeled and thinly sliced (75g)
- 1 cup bell pepper, thinly sliced (140g)
- Fresh herbs (green onions, mint), to taste (15g)
- Juice of 1 lime (30-45ml)
- 2 tbsp soy sauce (30ml)
- 1 tsp honey (7g)
- 1 tsp mustard (5g)
- 2 chicken breasts (300g)
- 1 cup cooked wild rice (180g)
- Salt and pepper, to taste.

Instructions:

1. Season the chicken breast with salt and pepper. Heat a grill or skillet over medium-high heat and cook the chicken until it's cooked through, about 5-7 minutes per side. Make sure it's no longer pink in the center. Remove from heat and let it rest for a few minutes before slicing it into thin strips.
2. In a small bowl, whisk together lime juice, soy sauce, honey, and mustard to create the dressing.
3. In a large bowl, combine cooked wild rice, sliced carrots, thinly sliced bell pepper, and half of the dressing. Toss well to combine.
4. Arrange the rice and vegetable mixture on a serving plate. Top with the sliced grilled chicken.
5. Drizzle the remaining dressing over the salad.
6. Garnish with chopped fresh herbs like green onions and mint.

Nutritional Information (Per Serving): Calories: 300 | Fat: 21g | Protein: 29g | Carbohydrates: 38g | Sugars: 16g | Fiber: 9g | Sodium: 674mg

Thai Minced Chicken Salad

Prep: 15 minutes | Cook: 10 minutes | Serves: 2

Ingredients:

- 1 1/3 cups minced chicken (300g)
- 1/2 cup zucchini (100g)
- 2 cloves garlic (6g)
- 2 tsp ginger (10g)
- 1/4 cup red onion (50g)
- 2 tbsp vegetable oil (30ml)
- 4 tsp soy sauce (20ml)
- 1 cup butterhead lettuce (50g)
- 2 tbsp pecan nuts (10g)
- 1 tbsp red chili pepper (10g)

Instructions:

1. Finely dice garlic and ginger. Peel and finely chop the red onion.
2. Heat vegetable oil in a skillet. Add diced ginger, garlic, and red onion. Sauté over medium heat for 1 minute until they turn golden brown.
3. Add minced chicken to the skillet. Cook, stirring constantly, until the chicken changes color and becomes white, about 3-4 minutes.
4. Pour in soy sauce. Mix well and cook over medium heat until the liquid evaporates. Keep stirring occasionally.
5. Prepare the zucchini by washing it thoroughly and cutting it into small cubes. Add the zucchini to the skillet with the chicken mixture. Cook for 2 minutes. The zucchini should remain slightly crunchy.
6. Prepare the red chili pepper by slicing it into thin circles. Roughly chop the pecan nuts.
7. Wash and dry the butterhead lettuce leaves. Arrange them on a serving plate.
8. Place the cooked chicken and zucchini mixture on top of the lettuce leaves.
9. Sprinkle the salad with pecan nuts and red chili pepper circles.

Nutritional Information (Per Serving): Calories: 350 | Fat: 24g | Protein: 24g | Carbohydrates: 13g | Sugars: 5g | Fiber: 3g | Sodium: 1034mg

Grilled Chicken and Eggplant Salad

Prep: 10 minutes | Cook: 10 minutes | Serves: 2

Ingredients:

- 1 cup chicken breast, sliced into strips (250g)
- 1 tsp honey (7g)
- 2.5 tbsp olive oil (37.5ml)
- 1 tsp mixed dry herbs
- 2 cups eggplant, diced (270g)
- 1/2 cup carrot, julienned (50g)
- 1/2 tsp balsamic vinegar (2.5ml)
- 3 cups mixed salad greens (150g)
- 1/2 tsp curry powder

Instructions:

1. In a bowl, combine chicken strips with honey, 1 tbsp olive oil, curry powder, and mixed dry herbs. Mix well and let it marinate for 5-7 minutes.
2. Heat a grill pan or a regular skillet. Grill the marinated chicken strips for 3-5 minutes until cooked through. Transfer to a plate.
3. In the same pan, add 0.5 tbsp olive oil and diced eggplant. Stir and grill for 3-5 minutes until tender.
4. Add julienned carrot to the pan with eggplant. Stir and cook for 1 more minute. Drizzle with balsamic vinegar, mix well, and remove from heat.
5. In a salad bowl, arrange the mixed salad greens. Drizzle with the remaining olive oil.
6. Top the salad greens with the grilled chicken strips, eggplant, and carrot mixture while still warm.
7. Optionally, sprinkle with chopped nuts (such as pistachios) before serving.

Nutritional Information (Per Serving): Calories: 280 | Fat: 18g | Protein: 23g | Carbohydrates: 20g | Sugars: 11g | Fiber: 7g | Sodium: 315mg

Eggplant, Pepper, and Green Buckwheat Salad

Prep: 15 minutes | Cook: 20 minutes | Serves: 4

Ingredients:

- 3 eggplants, diced (550g each, so 1650g total)
- 2 sweet peppers, thinly sliced (each 150g)
- 1 white onion, sliced (150g)
- 3 cloves of garlic, minced (about 9g)
- 3 tbsp green buckwheat (27g)
- 3 tbsp soy sauce (45ml)
- 2 tbsp vegetable oil (30ml)
- 2 tbsp lemon juice (30ml)
- 1 tsp honey (7g)
- 3 tbsp fresh herbs (parsley, cilantro, or mint), finely chopped (11.25g)

Instructions:

1. Cook the green buckwheat according to the package instructions. Drain any excess water and set aside.
2. Place diced eggplants on a flat plate and microwave for 5-6 minutes at 800W, or until tender.

Alternatively, you can boil the eggplants in water until tender.

3. In a mixing bowl, combine the cooked eggplants, sweet peppers, sliced onion, and minced garlic.

4. In another bowl, prepare the dressing by mixing soy sauce, vegetable oil, lemon juice, honey, and minced garlic.

5. Pour the dressing over the vegetables and toss well to combine.

6. Add the cooked green buckwheat and fresh herbs to the salad. Mix gently to combine all ingredients evenly.

7. Taste the salad and adjust the seasoning if needed, adding more lemon juice or soy sauce according to your preference.

8. Serve immediately or refrigerate for about 5 hours to allow the flavors to meld.

Nutritional Information (Per Serving): Calories: 180 | Fat: 8g | Protein: 4g | Carbohydrates: 29g | Sugars: 8g | Fiber: 7g | Sodium: 682mg

Spicy Eggplant Salad

Prep: 25 minutes | Cook: 15 minutes | Serves: 4

Ingredients:

- 2 eggplants (each 550g, so about 1100g total)
- 2 fresh cucumbers (600g)
- 2 pickled cucumbers (200g)
- 1 red onion (about 150g)
- 1 tsp lemon juice (about 5ml)
- 4 tbsp vegetable oil (60ml)
- 1.5 tsp salt
- Black pepper, to taste

Instructions:

1. Wash the eggplants, cut them into slices, and then each slice into 4 parts.

2. Place eggplant pieces in a bowl, sprinkle with 1 tsp of salt, mix, and let sit for 10–15 minutes.

3. Thinly slice the red onion into half rings. Add 0.25 tsp of salt and 1-2 tsp of lemon juice to the onion. Mix and let the onion marinate.

4. Squeeze out excess liquid from the eggplants using your hands and transfer them to a separate bowl.

5. Heat 3 tbsp of vegetable oil in a pan and add the squeezed eggplants. Fry for 10–15 minutes, stirring occasionally.

6. Transfer the fried eggplants to a paper towel to absorb excess oil.

7. Dice both fresh and pickled cucumbers into small cubes.

8. In a bowl, combine fresh and pickled cucumbers, season with salt to taste, add the marinated onion, fried eggplants, black pepper, and a tablespoon of vegetable oil. Mix the salad well.

9. Transfer the finished salad to a serving bowl, garnish with herbs if desired.

Nutritional Information (Per Serving): Calories: 175 | Fat: 15g | Protein: 3g | Carbohydrates: 27g | Sugars: 11g | Fiber: 7g | Sodium: 678mg

Baked Eggplant, Tomato, and Feta Salad

Prep: 15 minutes | Cook: 15 minutes | Serves: 4

Ingredients:

- 2 cups eggplant, sliced (350g)
- 1 1/2 cups tomatoes, halved (220g)
- 2 cups mixed salad greens (60g)
- 1 cup feta cheese, cubed (120g)
- 4 tbsp vegetable oil (60ml)
- 2 cloves garlic, minced (6g)
- 1 tbsp lemon juice (15ml)
- 2 tbsp fresh basil, chopped (5g)
- Salt, mixed pepper, to taste

Instructions:

1. Sprinkle the eggplant slices with salt and let them sit for 10–15 minutes. Rinse and squeeze out excess moisture.

2. Preheat the oven to 180°C (350°F). Arrange the eggplant slices on a baking sheet lined with parchment paper and bake for about 15 minutes.

3. Prepare the marinade by blending basil, minced garlic, and three tablespoons of oil.

4. Pour the marinade over the baked eggplant and let it marinate until cooled completely.

5. Divide the salad greens onto plates or arrange them on a large serving platter.

6. Drain excess marinade from the eggplant and place it on the salad greens.

7. Top with halved tomatoes and cubed feta cheese.

8. In the leftover marinade, add one tablespoon of oil, lemon juice, a pinch of sugar, and mix well. Adjust seasoning if needed.

9. Drizzle the dressing evenly over the salad.

10. Sprinkle the baked eggplant, tomato, and feta salad with mixed pepper. Serve immediately.

Nutritional Information (Per Serving): Calories: 267 | Fat: 21g | Protein: 6g | Carbohydrates: 13g | Sugars: 6g | Fiber: 5g | Sodium: 430mg

Korean-Style Eggplant Salad

Prep: 30 minutes | Cook: 7 minutes | Serves: 4

Ingredients:

- 3 cups young eggplants, thinly sliced (450g)
- 2 sweet bell peppers (about 2 cups, 300g total)
- 1 medium carrot (about 1/2 cup, 61g)
- 3 tbsp olive oil (45ml)
- 1 medium red onion (about 1 cup, 150g)
- 1 tsp sugar (4g)
- 4 cloves garlic (12g)
- 1 tbsp sesame seeds (9g)
- 0.75 tbsp vinegar (9%) (11ml)
- 1 tsp coriander ((2g)
- 3 tbsp soy sauce (45ml)
- 1/2 tsp black pepper (1g)
- Fresh herbs (cilantro, parsley, etc.), to taste (approximately 1/4 cup, 15g)
- Salt, to taste

Instructions:

1. Sprinkle eggplant slices with salt and let sit for 20 minutes. Rinse and pat dry with paper towels.

2. Cut sweet bell peppers into thin strips. Use a grater or a mandoline to cut the carrot into thin strips. Slice the red onion into thin half-rings.

3. Heat 1 tbsp olive oil in a pan over medium heat. Sauté eggplant slices for 6-7 minutes or until tender, using tongs to gently flip them. Remove from heat.

4. In a small bowl, mix 2 tbsp olive oil, sugar, soy sauce, vinegar, black pepper, crushed garlic, and ground coriander to make the dressing.

5. Toast sesame seeds in a dry pan until lightly golden.

6. In a large bowl, combine sautéed eggplants, sweet bell peppers, carrot, and red onion. Pour the dressing over the vegetables. Add toasted sesame seeds and fresh herbs. Adjust salt, pepper, and acidity to taste.

7. Refrigerate the salad for at least 1 hour or overnight before serving.

Nutritional Information (Per Serving): Calories: 192 | Fat: 11g | Protein: 2g | Carbohydrates: 12g | Sugars: 6g | Fiber: 3g | Sodium: 439mg

Salad with Orange, Avocado, and Mozzarella

Prep: 15 minutes | Cook: 0 minutes | Serves: 2

Ingredients:

- 1 cup mozzarella cheese (120g)
- 1 large orange (200g)
- 1 1/2 cups cucumber (250g)
- 1/2 medium avocado (100g)
- 2 cups iceberg lettuce (70g)
- 1 cup basil leaves (30g)
- 1 tbsp vegetable oil
- 2 tbsp orange juice
- 1 tsp lemon juice
- 1/2 tsp grain mustard
- 1/2 tsp honey
- Pinch of salt

Instructions:

1. Rinse lettuce and basil leaves under running water and let excess water drain. Tear iceberg lettuce into bite-sized pieces.

2. Prepare the orange dressing for the salad. In a bowl, mix vegetable oil, lemon juice, orange juice, half a teaspoon of honey, grain mustard, and a pinch of salt. Mix until well combined.

3. Rinse the cucumber. If the skin is thick, peel it partially, leaving some stripes for texture. Slice the cucumber into even rounds.

4. Peel the orange, removing the white parts, and cut it into small pieces.

5. Peel and pit the avocado, cutting it into medium pieces. Add lemon juice to prevent browning.

6. Cut mozzarella cheese into small cubes.

7. In a large bowl, combine lettuce, cucumber rounds, orange pieces, avocado, and mozzarella cheese.

8. Drizzle the prepared orange dressing over the salad and toss gently to combine.

9. Garnish the salad with fresh basil leaves.

Nutritional Information (Per Serving): Calories: 372 | Fat: 27g | Protein: 17g | Carbohydrates: 22g | Sugars: 12g | Fiber: 6g | Sodium: 630mg

Apricot and Soft Cheese Salad

Prep: 10 minutes | Cook: 0 minutes | Serves: 2

Ingredients:

- 1 cup apricots, pitted and sliced (200g)
- 3/4 cup cottage cheese (150g)
- 1/4 cup nectarine, sliced (50g)
- 1/2 cup cucumber, thinly sliced (50g)
- 1 cup lettuce leaves (50g)
- 1 tsp lemon juice
- 1 tsp grain mustard
- 1 tsp honey
- 1 tsp vegetable oil
- 1 sprig of basil
- Pinch of salt

Instructions:

1. Prepare the dressing: combine vegetable oil, grain mustard, lemon juice, and honey. Add a pinch of salt. Mix well.

2. Arrange torn lettuce leaves on a plate.

3. Place apricots, nectarine, and cucumber on the lettuce.

4. Add cottage cheese, then blueberries.

5. Garnish with basil leaves.

6. Drizzle with the dressing before serving.

Nutritional Information (Per Serving): Calories: 245 | Fat: 11g | Protein: 12g | Carbohydrates: 27g | Sugars: 19g | Fiber: 4g | Sodium: 345mg

Mango Salad

Prep: 10 minutes | Cook: 0 minutes | Serves: 2

Ingredients:

- 1 green mango, thinly sliced (200g)
- 1/2 red onion, finely sliced (70g)
- 1/2 yellow bell pepper, thinly sliced (about 100g)
- 5 sprigs parsley, finely chopped (10g)
- 1 tsp lemon juice (5ml)
- Pinch of salt
- Optional: a few drops of Worcestershire sauce
- 1/2 tsp olive oil (2.5ml)
- 1 tbsp almond flakes (10g)

Instructions:

1. Slice the mango into thin, long strips using a mandoline or a julienne peeler. No need to peel the mango; grate it on all sides until you reach the pit.

2. Use a serrated knife or a special slicer for even mango slices.

3. Choose any color of sweet pepper: yellow, red, green, or orange. If you prefer a bit of spice, add some finely chopped chili pepper.

4. Slice half of a small red onion very thin. If the onion is too sharp, you can marinate it for 5–10 minutes or soak it in water to reduce its pungency.

5. Finely chop the parsley. You can use scissors for this step.

6. Combine all the ingredients in a salad bowl and drizzle with lemon juice. Use a little lemon juice if the mango is already tangy; use a bit more if it's not very ripe. The salad should have a slightly tangy taste. If desired, add a few drops of Worcestershire sauce.

7. Mix all the ingredients and drizzle with olive oil.

8. Divide the salad between two plates and sprinkle with almond flakes.

9. Let the salad sit for about 15 minutes before serving.

Nutritional Information (Per Serving): Calories: 120 | Fat: 2g | Protein: 2g | Carbohydrates: 27g | Sugars: 20g | Fiber: 4g | Sodium: 117mg

Persimmon and Mozzarella Salad

Prep: 10 minutes | Cook: 0 minutes | Serves: 2

Ingredients:

- 1 ripe persimmon (approximately 200g)
- 100g mozzarella cheese
- 1 pack of mixed salad greens (2 cups, 50g)
- 50g olives (pitted)
- Fresh herbs, (5g)
- Salt, to taste
- Black pepper, to taste
- 0.5 tsp olive oil (2.5ml)

Instructions:

1. Wash and pat dry the salad greens and persimmon. Tear the greens and arrange them on a plate.
2. Cut the persimmon in half, remove the stem and seeds, and dice the flesh into medium-sized cubes. Scatter them over the greens.
3. Cut the mozzarella in half or into chunks if using larger pieces. Arrange it on the plate alongside the persimmon.
4. Slice the olives in half vertically and place them on the salad.
5. Finely chop green onions and dill and sprinkle them over the salad.
6. Season the salad with salt and black pepper, then drizzle with olive oil.
7. Serve immediately, preserving the nutrients and vibrant flavors of the salad.

Nutritional Information (Per Serving): Calories: 200 | Fat: 13g | Protein: 11g | Carbohydrates: 15g | Sugars: 7g | Fiber: 2g | Sodium: 428mg

Italian Orzo Salad with Basil

Prep: 10 minutes | Cook: 2 minutes | Serves: 2

Ingredients:

- 2 cucumbers (450g each)
- 2 tomatoes (different colors) (180g each)
- 1/2 bell pepper (100g)
- 5 sprigs basil (5g)
- 1/2 cup orzo pasta (200ml)
- 1 tsp olive oil
- Salt, to taste
- 1 tsp pesto (optional)
- 1/2 tsp lemon juice (optional)

Instructions:

1. Cook orzo according to package instructions (usually 2 minutes). Drain and rinse under cold water. Place in a mixing bowl.
2. Dice cucumbers, tomatoes, and bell pepper into small pieces. Add them to the bowl with orzo.
3. Finely chop the basil leaves. Add them to the bowl with the vegetables and orzo.
4. Mix all the ingredients, drizzle with olive oil, and add salt to taste.
5. Optionally, add 1 tsp of pesto for extra flavor and a splash of lemon juice for brightness.
6. Mix the salad thoroughly, transfer to a serving bowl.

Nutritional Information (Per Serving): Calories: 250 | Fat: 13g | Protein: 11g | Carbohydrates: 15g | Sugars: 7g | Fiber: 2g | Sodium: 428mg

Spinach, Cherry Tomato, and Parmesan Salad

Prep: 15 minutes | Cook: 0 minutes | Serves: 2

Ingredients:

- 2 cups spinach leaves (50g)
- 1 1/2 cups cherry tomatoes (200g)
- 1 medium cucumber (120g)
- 1 tbsp Parmesan cheese, grated (5g)
- 3 tbsp olive oil (45ml)
- 1 tbsp balsamic vinegar (15ml)
- 1/2 tsp honey (3.5g)
- 1/2 tsp mustard (2.5g)

Instructions:

1. Wash the spinach leaves thoroughly and pat them dry.
2. Slice the cucumber into thin rounds.
3. Cut the cherry tomatoes into quarters.
4. In a salad bowl, combine the spinach leaves, cucumber slices, and cherry tomatoes.
5. In a small bowl, whisk together olive oil, balsamic vinegar, honey, mustard, salt, and black pepper until well combined.
6. Drizzle the dressing over the salad and toss gently to coat the ingredients evenly.

7. Sprinkle grated Parmesan cheese over the salad as a finishing touch.

8. Serve the salad immediately, ensuring it's well-mixed just before serving.

Nutritional Information (Per Serving): Calories: 230 | Fat: 18g | Protein: 2g | Carbohydrates: 12g | Sugars: 7g | Fiber: 2g | Sodium: 160mg

Seaweed Salad with Egg and Potato

Prep: 20 minutes | Cook: 30 minutes | Serves: 2

Ingredients:

- 5.3 ounces (150g) frozen seaweed
- 5.3 ounces (150g) boiled potatoes
- 3 boiled eggs
- 0.5 (50g) red onion, thinly sliced
- 5.3 ounces (150g) mussels
- 1 tsp olive oil (for sautéing)
- 1.5 tsp olive oil (for dressing)
- 1 tsp Dijon mustard
- 1 tsp lemon juice
- Pinch of salt
- Black pepper, to taste

Instructions:

1. In a pan, sauté the sliced red onion in 1 teaspoon of olive oil. Add the mussels and cook for 2-3 minutes. Remove from heat.

2. In a small bowl, whisk together the Dijon mustard, 1.5 teaspoons of olive oil, lemon juice, a pinch of salt, and black pepper to create the dressing.

3. Combine the boiled eggs, boiled potatoes, frozen seaweed, sautéed onion, and mussels in a large bowl.

4. Drizzle the dressing over the salad and toss gently to coat the ingredients evenly.

5. Adjust the salt and add more black pepper if desired.

6. Garnish with slices of boiled egg and mussels.

7. Mix well and serve immediately.

Nutritional Information (Per Serving): Calories: 230 | Fat: 18g | Protein: 2g | Carbohydrates: 12g | Sugars: 7g | Fiber: 2g | Sodium: 160mg

Red Cabbage and Green Pea Salad

Prep: 20 minutes | Cook: 0 minutes | Serves: 4

Ingredients:

- 2 1/2 cups red cabbage (400g)
- 1 1/2 cups canned green peas (340g)
- 1 onion (150g)
- 6 sprigs of parsley (20g)
- Salt, to taste
- Ground black pepper, to taste
- 1.5 tbsp lemon juice (22.5ml)
- 3 tbsp sunflower oil (45ml)

Instructions:

1. Peel, wash, and dice the onion. Place in a bowl, add lemon juice, a pinch of salt, and mix. Let it marinate for 15–20 minutes.

2. Remove outer leaves of the red cabbage. Rinse and pat dry. Slice thinly. Sprinkle with a bit of salt and massage the cabbage to soften it.

3. Combine marinated onion, cabbage, drained green peas in a salad bowl. Mix in finely chopped parsley.

4. Season with salt and pepper to taste. Drizzle with sunflower oil.

5. Toss the salad gently to combine all the ingredients. Serve immediately as a side dish or on its own.

Nutritional Information (Per Serving): Calories: 180 |Fat: 9g | Protein: 3g | Carbohydrates: 14g | Sugars: 4g | Fiber: 4g | Sodium: 240mg

Light Salad with Napa Cabbage and Corn

Prep: 15 minutes | Cook: 0 minutes | Serves: 4

Ingredients:

- 21.2 ounces Napa cabbage (600g)
- 1 can of corn kernels (432g)
- 2 carrots (100g)
- 1/2 cup green onions (40g)
- 2 cloves of garlic (6g)
- 3 tbsp dill (4.5g)
- 2 tbsp lemon juice (30ml)
- 4 tbsp vegetable oil (60ml)
- Salt, to taste.

Instructions:

1. Chop dill (remove coarse stems). Wash, peel, and grate carrots. Finely chop green onions. Drain water from corn if canned.
2. Slightly squeeze Napa cabbage and place it in a bowl. Add corn, grated carrots, green onions, and chopped dill.
3. Peel and finely chop garlic cloves. In a jar, combine garlic, vegetable oil, salt, sugar, lemon juice. Close the lid and shake well until the dressing is homogeneous.
4. Pour the dressing over the salad right before serving. Mix gently.

Nutritional Information (Per Serving): Calories: 210 | Fat: 13g | Protein: 2g | Carbohydrates: 20g | Sugars: 6g | Fiber: 4g | Sodium: 335mg

Colorful Salad with Yogurt and Cilantro Dressing

Prep: 15 minutes | Cook: 0 minutes | Serves: 4

Ingredients:

- 1 1/2 cups iceberg lettuce (200g)
- 2 cups cherry tomatoes, halved (300g)
- 1 cup red bell pepper, diced (150g)
- 1/4 cup green onions, chopped (30g)
- 2 1/4 cups canned red kidney beans (400g)
- 1 1/2 cups canned corn kernels (340g)
- 1 whole bunch cilantro (25g)
- 3/4 cup yogurt (200g)
- 1 large garlic clove (5g)
- 2 tbsp lemon or lime juice (30ml)
- Salt, to taste

Instructions:

1. Tear or chop iceberg lettuce into a large bowl. Add halved cherry tomatoes, drained kidney beans, corn kernels, diced red bell pepper, and chopped green onions.
2. In a blender, combine yogurt, whole cilantro bunch, freshly pressed garlic clove, lemon or lime juice, and salt. Blend until smooth and creamy.
3. Dress the salad with the yogurt and cilantro dressing just before serving. Mix well.

Nutritional Information (Per Serving): Calories: 220 | Fat: 2g | Protein: 7g | Carbohydrates: 32g | Sugars: 6g | Fiber: 7g | Sodium: 283mg

Roasted Cauliflower Salad

Prep: 10 minutes | Cook: 25 minutes | Serves: 2

Ingredients:

- 3 cups cauliflower, broken into florets (400g)
- 1/2 cup red bell pepper, sliced (100g)
- 1/2 cup red onion, sliced (80g)
- 2 tbsp olive oil (30ml)
- 1/2 tsp balsamic vinegar (2.5ml)
- 1/2 tsp salt
- 1 tsp honey (7g)
- 1/2 tbsp apple cider vinegar (7.5ml)
- 2 cups arugula (or other leafy greens) (50g)
- Pumpkin seeds, to taste (variable, 10g)

Instructions:

1. Preheat the oven to 180°C (350°F). In a baking dish, combine cauliflower florets, red bell pepper slices, and red onion slices. Drizzle with half of the olive oil and sprinkle with half of the salt. Toss to coat evenly. Roast in the preheated oven for 25 minutes.
2. In a small bowl, whisk together the remaining olive oil, balsamic vinegar, honey, apple cider vinegar, and a pinch of salt.
3. In a salad bowl, place washed and dried arugula. Top with the roasted vegetables. Drizzle the dressing over the salad just before serving.
4. Sprinkle the salad with pumpkin seeds for extra crunch and nutrition.

Nutritional Information (Per Serving): Calories: 250 | Fat: 14g | Protein: 3g | Carbohydrates: 21g | Sugars: 10g | Fiber: 5g | Sodium: 367mg

Rice and Cucumber Salad

Prep: 10 minutes | Cook: 15 minutes | Serves: 2

Ingredients:

- 1 cup cooked Basmati rice (250 ml)
- 1 cucumber, diced (300g)
- Green onions, to taste
- Dill, to taste
- 2 tbsp olive oil (30ml)
- 2 tbsp lemon juice (30ml)
- 1 pinch of salt
- 1 pinch of black pepper

Instructions:

1. Cook the rice using the Jamie Oliver method: place rice in a saucepan, add a pinch of salt, and pour boiling water in a 1:2 ratio (rice to water). Add 1 tablespoon of olive oil, cover with a lid, and cook on low heat for no more than 15 minutes.
2. In a small bowl, mix olive oil, lemon juice, salt, and black pepper to make the sauce.
3. Let the rice cool completely, as you prepare the other ingredients.
4. Dice the cucumber, chop green onions, and dill.
5. Mix the cooled rice with the cucumber, green onions, and dill. Pour the sauce over the salad and toss to combine.

Nutritional Information (Per Serving): Calories: 280 | Fat: 9g | Protein: 3g | Carbohydrates: 14g | Sugars: 4g | Fiber: 4g | Sodium: 240mg

Grilled Pepper and Mushroom Salad

Prep: 10 minutes | Cook: 10 minutes | Serves: 2

Ingredients:

- 0.5 red sweet pepper, sliced (75g)
- 10 mushrooms, halved (50g)
- 1 handful of olives (30g)
- Salt, to taste
- 1.5 tbsp vegetable oil (22.5ml)
- Spices, to taste
- 40g Feta cheese
- 5 sprigs of parsley (5g)

Instructions:

1. Slice the red pepper into long strips. Cut mushrooms in half for easy grilling. Place them in a bowl.
2. Add a tablespoon of vegetable oil to the vegetables. Season with salt and spices according to your preference. Mix well.
3. Grill the peppers and mushrooms over charcoal for about 8–10 minutes until the edges of the peppers are slightly charred. Keep an eye on them to prevent burning.
4. Remove the vegetables from the heat and let them cool slightly. Peel the skin off the peppers when they are comfortable to touch. Slice the peppers into strips. If using large mushrooms, cut them in half again.
5. Finely chop the parsley. Cut the olives in half.
6. In a bowl, combine peppers, mushrooms, parsley, and olives. Drizzle with a bit of olive oil and toss.
7. Transfer the salad to a flat dish. Crumble Feta cheese on top. The cheese is salty, so no need for additional seasoning.
8. Serve the grilled pepper and mushroom salad warm or cold, perfect as a side to grilled meats or fish.

Nutritional Information (Per Serving): Calories: 180 | Fat: 10g | Protein: 4g | Carbohydrates: 12g | Sugars: 2g | Fiber: 4g | Sodium: 300mg

Tabbouleh Salad with Couscous

Prep: 15 minutes | Cook: 5 minutes | Serves: 2

Ingredients:

- 0.25 cup couscous (200 ml)
- 0.5 cup water (200 ml)
- 1 small tomato (100g)
- 1 small cucumber (150g)
- 0.25 bell pepper (37.5g)
- Vegetable oil, to taste
- 5 sprigs of parsley (5g)
- 1 sprig of mint (1g)
- 1 handful of green onions (30g)
- Lemon juice, to taste
- Salt, to taste

Instructions:

1. Pour boiling water over couscous and let it sit, covered, until all water is absorbed. Fluff with a fork.

2. Finely dice cucumber, bell pepper, and tomato. Remove seeds and excess moisture from the tomato.

3. Finely chop parsley, mint, and green onions.

4. In a bowl, combine couscous, diced vegetables, and chopped herbs.

5. Season with salt. Drizzle with vegetable oil and add lemon juice to taste. Toss everything together until well combined.

6. Serve the Tabbouleh Salad with Couscous on flatbreads or in a salad bowl.

Nutritional Information (Per Serving): Calories: 120 | Fat: 2g | Protein: 5g | Carbohydrates: 42g | Sugars: 3g | Fiber: 4g | Sodium: 200mg

Zucchini and Tomato Salad

Prep: 15 minutes | Cook: 5 minutes | Serves: 4

Ingredients:

- 2 zucchinis (400g)
- 6 tomatoes (1080g)
- 2 carrots (about 122g)
- 3 tbsp sour cream (45g)
- 0.5 cup flour (200 ml)
- Salt, to taste
- Optional: garlic
- 50 ml vegetable oil

Instructions:

1. Slice zucchinis, sprinkle with salt, and toss. Coat zucchini slices in flour by shaking them in a container with flour.

2. Heat vegetable oil in a pan. Quickly fry zucchini slices for about 2 minutes on each side. Place fried zucchinis on a paper towel to remove excess oil.

3. Peel and grate carrots using a coarse grater.

4. Slice tomatoes into rounds just before assembling the salad to retain their juice.

5. Layer the salad on a plate: lettuce leaves, fried zucchinis, grated carrots, sour cream sauce, tomato rounds.

6. Optional: Add Garlic. If desired, mix minced garlic into the sour cream sauce.

7. Garnish the Zucchini and Tomato Salad with your favorite herbs and serve.

Nutritional Information (Per Serving): Calories: 210 | Fat: 12g | Protein: 3g | Carbohydrates: 18g | Sugars: 6g | Fiber: 3g | Sodium: 220mg

Zucchini, Soft Cheese, Avocado, and Walnut Salad

Prep: 10 minutes | Cook: 5 minutes | Serves: 2

Ingredients:

- 1 1/2 cups soft cheese (150g)
- 1/2 cup walnuts (50g)
- 1 1/2 cups avocado (150g)
- 2 cups zucchini (200g)
- 2 tbsp olive oil (30ml)
- 1 tbsp lemon juice (15ml)
- 2 sprigs of thyme (1g)
- Pinch of salt

Instructions:

1. Rinse, trim the ends, and slice zucchini into 1-centimeter thick circles.

2. Heat a grill pan over medium heat and brush it with vegetable oil. Grill zucchini slices on both sides until tender and slightly golden. Adjust the cooking time to achieve desired tenderness.

3. In a small bowl, combine olive oil, lemon juice, thyme leaves, and a pinch of salt. Mix well to create the dressing.

4. Peel and slice the avocado. Sprinkle the slices with lemon juice to prevent browning.

5. Arrange grilled zucchini, soft cheese, avocado slices, and walnuts on a plate or divide them into individual servings.

6. Drizzle the olive oil and lemon dressing over the salad.

7. Garnish with extra thyme leaves if desired and serve immediately.

Nutritional Information (Per Serving): Calories: 420 | Fat: 36g | Protein: 12g | Carbohydrates: 17g | Sugars: 3g | Fiber: 10g | Sodium: 180mg

Arugula, Stracciatella, and Tomato Salad

Prep: 10 minutes | Cook: 0 minutes | Serves: 2

Ingredients:

- 1/2 cup Stracciatella cheese (100g)
- 1/4 cup arugula leaves (30g)
- 1 1/4 cups tomatoes (300g)
- 1 tbsp olive oil (about 15ml)
- Pinch of salt
- Pinch of black pepper

Instructions:

1. Slice the tomatoes into 1 cm thick slices. Arrange them in a circular pattern on a serving plate.
2. Spread Stracciatella cheese evenly over the tomatoes.
3. Sprinkle arugula leaves on top, removing any thick stems. Rinse arugula thoroughly if using soil-grown variety to avoid dirt.
4. Drizzle the salad with olive oil. Use a small amount, just enough to lightly coat the ingredients.
5. Sprinkle freshly ground black pepper and a pinch of sea salt over the salad. The salt will enhance the sweetness of the tomatoes.

Nutritional Information (Per Serving): Calories: 250 | Fat: 19g | Protein: 8g | Carbohydrates: 10g | Sugars: 5g | Fiber: 3g | Sodium: 270mg

Mussels, Arugula, and Cherry Tomato Salad

Prep: 15 minutes | Cook: 5 minutes | Serves: 2

Ingredients:

- 1 cup mussels (200g)
- 1/2 cup cherry tomatoes (120g)
- 1 cup arugula (50g)
- 1 bell pepper (150g)
- 1/2 red onion (75g)
- Seasoning, to taste
- 2 cloves of garlic (6g)
- 2 tbsp pesto (30g)
- 1 tbsp balsamic vinegar (15ml)
- 4 tbsp olive oil (60ml)
- Optional: salad greens (variable amount)

Instructions:

1. Sauté mussels with garlic, Provencal herbs, and 1 tbsp olive oil for 2 minutes. Let cool.
2. Sauté bell pepper, halve cherry tomatoes, and slice red onion.
3. Prepare Dressing: Mix pesto, balsamic vinegar, and 3 tbsp olive oil.
4. Place arugula, tomatoes, bell pepper, and mussels on a plate.
5. Drizzle with pesto dressing. Top with red onion rings.

Nutritional Information (Per Serving): Calories: 350 | Fat: 31g | Protein: 13g | Carbohydrates: 22g | Sugars: 8g | Fiber: 4g | Sodium: 480mg

Tuna and Arugula Salad with Pomegranate Sauce

Prep: 15 minutes | Cook: 2 minutes | Serves: 2

Ingredients:

- 1 cup tuna fillet (150g)
- 1 cup arugula (50g)
- 1 cup tomatoes (150g)
- 1/2 cup avocado (100g)
- 1/2 tsp sesame seeds
- Pinch of salt
- Juice of 3 lemon wedges (15ml)
- 1.5 tbsp olive oil (15ml)
- 1 tbsp Pomegranate Molasses (15ml)
- Pinch of mixed peppers

Instructions:

1. Marinate tuna fillet with lemon juice for 10 minutes. Heat a pan over high heat, add a bit of olive oil, and sear the tuna for 1 minute on each side. Slice the tuna into even pieces.
2. Rinse arugula and pat dry. Arrange it on a plate.
3. Wash and slice the tomatoes, and cut the avocado into chunks. Place them on the arugula. Squeeze lemon juice over the avocado to prevent browning.
4. Drizzle olive oil over the salad, season with salt and mixed peppers.
5. Sprinkle sesame seeds on top of the tuna slices.

6. Serve the tuna slices on the prepared arugula, tomatoes, and avocado. Drizzle with pomegranate molasses.

Nutritional Information (Per Serving): Calories: 280 | Fat: 21g | Protein: 25g | Carbohydrates: 20g | Sugars: 7g | Fiber: 6g | Sodium: 380mg

Salmon and Avocado Salad

Prep: 15 minutes | Cook: 2 minutes | Serves: 2

Ingredients:

- 7 oz lightly salted salmon, cubed (200g)
- 2 small avocados (300g)
- 1/2 cup apple (80g)
- 0.9 oz arugula (25g)
- 0.5 oz pine nuts (15g)
- 3.5 oz cherry tomatoes (100g)
- 1/4 cup hard cheese, grated (25g)
- 4 tbsp olive oil (about 60ml)
- 1 tbsp soy sauce (15ml)
- 1 tbsp apple cider vinegar (15ml)
- Black pepper to taste

Instructions:

1. Cube the salmon after removing the skin.
2. Grate the hard cheese finely.
3. Wash and pat dry the arugula leaves.
4. Rinse the cherry tomatoes, dry them, and cut into quarters or halves depending on their size.
5. In a small jar, combine soy sauce, apple cider vinegar, and olive oil. Close the lid and shake well to make the dressing.
6. Cut the avocados in half, remove the pits, scoop out the flesh, and cut it into 0.4-0.6 inch (1-1.5 cm) cubes.
7. Peel and cut the apple into small cubes (approximately 0.3-0.4 inch or 0.7-1 cm).
8. In a bowl, mix arugula, salmon, cherry tomatoes, apple cubes, and about 2/3 of the grated cheese. Season with black pepper to taste. Note: If your salmon and cheese are salty, you may not need to add extra salt.
9. Pour the dressing over the salad and gently toss to combine.
10. Sprinkle the salad with the remaining grated cheese and pine nuts.

Nutritional Information (Per Serving): Calories: 380 | Fat: 48g | Protein: 17g | Carbohydrates: 23g | Sugars: 9g | Fiber: 8g | Sodium: 660mg

Shrimp and Avocado Salad

Prep: 20 minutes | Cook: 15 minutes | Serves: 4

Ingredients:

- 2 large avocados (400g)
- 5.3 oz shrimp, cooked and chopped (150g)
- 5.3 oz smoked salmon, finely chopped (150g)
- 3 tomatoes (540g)
- Salt to taste
- 2 potatoes (300g)
- 2 limes (134g)
- 2 tbsp Greek yogurt (30g)
- 1 tsp finely chopped dill (1g)
- 1 lemon (for garnish) (58g)

Instructions:

1. Cook the shrimp, chop them, add finely chopped dill, and dress with Greek yogurt.
2. Finely chop the smoked salmon.
3. Cook the potatoes in their skins, cool, peel, mash with a fork, dress with the remaining sauce, season with salt to taste, and mix thoroughly.
4. Remove the core and seeds from the tomatoes. Dice the tomatoes into small pieces.
5. Cut the avocados, remove the pits, and peel. Cut into cubes, dress with lime juice, season with salt, and pepper.
6. When all the ingredients are ready, assemble the salad. Line a salad mold with plastic wrap (I used a deep form for baking Easter cakes).
7. Bottom layer – ½ part of the chopped avocado.
8. Next – shrimp. The following layer – salmon. Then another layer of avocado (the remaining part). Then tomatoes. Everything on top is covered with a layer of potatoes. Each layer is slightly compacted during assembly.

Nutritional Information (Per Serving): Calories: 320 | Fat: 25g | Protein: 20g | Carbohydrates: 30g | Sugars: 4g | Fiber: 8g | Sodium: 450mg

Shrimp Caesar Salad

Prep: 15 minutes | Cook: 10 minutes | Serves: 2

Ingredients:

- 10 tiger shrimp (200-300g for 10 shrimp)
- 2 tbsp Parmesan cheese (10g)
- 8 quail eggs
- 1 bunch of romaine lettuce (a bunch typically weighs about 200g)
- 2 tbsp lemon juice (30ml)
- 1/2 cup olive oil (120ml)
- 4 cloves of garlic (12g)
- 2 tbsp mayonnaise (30g)
- 2 anchovies (about 10g)
- 3 slices of Italian bread (preferably stale) (90g total)
- Freshly ground black pepper (to taste)
- 8 cherry tomatoes (160g)
- Salt to taste

Instructions:

1. Crush two cloves of garlic, mix with salt, freshly ground black pepper, and 3 tablespoons of olive oil. Cut the crusts off the Italian bread and dice into large cubes. Place the bread cubes in a bowl with the garlic oil mixture and toss to coat each piece. Arrange the bread cubes in a single layer in an ovenproof dish.
2. Bake the croutons in a preheated oven at 220°C (430°F) for 10 minutes until golden and crispy.
3. Peel and devein the shrimp, season with salt and pepper, and lightly drizzle with olive oil.
4. Blend the anchovies and remaining garlic clove in a blender. Add mayonnaise, lemon juice, and 1/4 cup of olive oil. Blend until smooth.
5. Boil the quail eggs, peel, and cut them in half lengthwise.
6. Grill the shrimp on a grill pan (or a regular pan without oil) until cooked through.
7. Wash and shake off excess water from the romaine lettuce. Tear it into large pieces and divide among the plates. Shave Parmesan cheese over the top using a vegetable peeler. Wash and dry the cherry tomatoes.
8. Drizzle the salad leaves with the prepared Caesar dressing. Top with the croutons, quail eggs, cherry tomatoes, and grilled shrimp.

Nutritional Information (Per Serving): Calories: 420 | Fat: 42g | Protein: 26g | Carbohydrates: 20g | Sugars: 3g | Fiber: 3g | Sodium: 1030mg

Calamari Salad with Egg and Fresh Cucumber

Prep: 15 minutes | Cook: 10 minutes | Serves: 4

Ingredients:

- 2 tbsp unsalted butter (for frying) (30g)
- 700g squid (frozen)
- 600g fresh mushrooms
- 3 fresh cucumbers (900g)
- 1 red bell pepper (150g)
- 4 eggs
- Black pepper to taste
- Salt to taste
- 5 tbsp mayonnaise (or your choice of dressing) (75g)
- 4 tbsp sour cream (or your choice of dressing) (60g)
- 2 tbsp soy sauce (or your choice of dressing) (30ml)
- 4 tbsp sesame oil (60ml)

Instructions:

1. Heat butter in a pan over high heat. Add mushrooms and fry until golden brown. Stir occasionally.
2. Place room temperature eggs in cold water, bring to a boil, then simmer for 5–7 minutes. Cool the eggs in ice-cold water and peel them. Cut into quarters.
3. Thaw the squid. Bring salted water to a boil. Cook the squid for no more than 5 minutes. Drain and cool.
4. Slice the squid into thin rings.
5. Wash the cucumbers, remove the ends, and slice them into thin strips using a vegetable peeler or a knife.
6. Wash the red bell pepper, remove the seeds, and slice it into thin half-rings.
7. Mix all the prepared ingredients together.
8. For the dressing, you can use mayonnaise mixed with soy sauce, or sour cream mixed with sesame oil. Season with salt and pepper according to your taste.
9. Drizzle the salad with the dressing and toss gently to combine.

Nutritional Information (Per Serving): Calories: 340 | Fat: 28g | Protein: 24g | Carbohydrates: 30g | Sugars: 6g | Fiber: 6g | Sodium: 680mg

CHAPTER 7: FISH AND SEAFOOD

Rice and Fish Burger

Prep: 30 minutes | Cook: 20 minutes | Serves: 2

Ingredients:

- 1 cup rice (150g)
- 7 oz fish fillet (200g, preferably Haddock)
- Cream cheese, to taste (amount varies)
- 3 lettuce leaves (a leaf of lettuce is approximately 10g, so about 30g total)
- 1 cucumber (300g)
- 2 eggs
- Sauce, to taste (Paprika-chili recommended)
- Spices for rice, optional (amount varies)
- Vegetable oil, for frying (amount varies)
- 2 tbsp all-purpose flour (16g)
- Bread crumbs, to taste (amount varies)

Instructions:

1. Cook rice with your choice of spices to form rice patties.
2. Separate egg yolks and whites. Mix egg whites with rice and add 2 tablespoons of flour. Mix well.
3. Cut fish into equal square pieces.
4. Use baking molds to shape rice buns. Place plastic wrap at the bottom, add rice mixture, and press down.
5. Dip fish in egg yolks and coat with bread crumbs. Fry in hot oil until golden brown.
6. Fry rice buns until crispy on both sides.
7. Spread cream cheese on the rice bun, place a lettuce leaf, add fried fish, and drizzle with sauce.
8. Add sliced cucumber on top of the fish.
9. Place the second rice bun on the cucumber.
10. Optionally, wrap the burger in seaweed and secure with a skewer for presentation.

Nutritional Information (Per Serving): Calories: 450 | Fat: 15g | Protein: 20g | Carbohydrates: 45g | Sugars: 3g | Fiber: 3g | Sodium: 480mg

Classic Seafood Paella

Prep: 20 minutes | Cook: 35 minutes | Serves: 4

Ingredients:

- 1 cup rice (200g)
- 2 1/2 cups water (600ml)
- 1/3 cup shallots, finely chopped (50g)
- 1 lime (67g)
- 1/2 cup tomatoes, diced (100g)
- 1/2 cup bell pepper, diced (100g)
- 1/2 cup green beans, trimmed (100g)
- 9 oz fish fillet (250g, preferably Sea Bass)
- 9 oz shrimp (250g)
- 3.5 oz mussels (100g)
- 3.5 oz squid (100g)
- 3.5 oz octopus (100g)
- 1/2 tsp saffron threads
- 1 sprig rosemary
- 3 tbsp olive oil (45ml)
- 1/2 tsp salt
- 2 pinches black pepper

Instructions:

1. Finely chop shallots, dice tomatoes, and cut bell pepper into small cubes.
2. Trim and cut green beans into halves.
3. Clean and cut fish fillet into small pieces.
4. Heat half of the olive oil in a pan. Add shallots and a sprig of rosemary. Cook until golden, then remove the rosemary.
5. Add diced bell pepper and tomatoes to the pan. Sauté for a few minutes.
6. Add green beans and cook for 1–2 minutes before adding rice. Stir for 2–3 minutes, then add the rest of the olive oil.
7. Pour in cold water, add salt, black pepper, and saffron. Cook the rice on low heat for about 15–18 minutes after boiling.
8. In another pan, heat olive oil and quickly sear the fish fillet for 1.5-2 minutes. Season with salt and set aside.
9. Prepare mussels, squid, and octopus for sautéing. Thaw, clean, and slice if needed. Sauté in olive oil for 1–2 minutes, then add salt.
10. Place the seafood on top of the almost-cooked rice. Let it simmer for 3–4 minutes with the lid on.

11. Add shrimp to the rice 3–4 minutes before finishing cooking. If the shrimp are raw, add them together with other seafood. It's crucial to prevent overcooking the shrimp.

12. Let the paella rest for 15–20 minutes. Before serving, cut lime into wedges and garnish the paella. Serve directly from the pan.

Nutritional Information (Per Serving): Calories: 430 | Fat: 16g | Protein: 40g | Carbohydrates: 63g | Sugars: 4g | Fiber: 4g | Sodium: 650mg

Squid and Egg Fried Rice

Prep: 10 minutes | Cook: 15 minutes | Serves: 2

Ingredients:

- 1/2 cup long-grain rice (100g)
- 1 small cooked squid (100-150g)
- 1/4 red onion (about 25g)
- 1/4 spicy red pepper or chili (adjust to taste) (10-15g)
- 4 sprigs dill (about 4g)
- 1.5 tsp vegetable oil (7.5ml)
- Salt, to taste
- 1 egg
- 1/2 garlic clove (1.5g)
- 1.5 tsp soy sauce (7.5ml)

Instructions:

1. Cook rice in salted water according to package instructions.

2. Finely chop onion, dill, garlic, and spicy red pepper.

3. Beat the egg in a bowl, add salt, and scramble in a hot skillet with a little vegetable oil until fully cooked and broken into small pieces.

4. In another skillet, heat the remaining vegetable oil and sauté onion, garlic, and spicy red pepper for a few minutes, stirring constantly to prevent burning.

5. Slice the cooked squid into rings, chop dill, and add both to the skillet along with the scrambled egg.

6. Drain the cooked rice and add it to the skillet. Pour in soy sauce and stir well to combine.

7. Taste and adjust salt if necessary.

8. Transfer the squid and egg fried rice to a plate. Optionally, sprinkle with toasted sesame seeds for extra flavor. Serve hot.

Nutritional Information (Per Serving): Calories: 380 | Fat: 8g | Protein: 17g | Carbohydrates: 58g | Sugars: 2g | Fiber: 2g | Sodium: 470mg

Asian Seafood Glass Noodles

Prep: 15 minutes | Cook: 10 minutes | Serves: 2

Ingredients:

- 3.5 oz (100g) glass noodles (bean thread vermicelli)
- 5.3 oz (150g) shrimp
- 5.3 oz (150g) mussels
- 1/4 red onion (25g)
- 1/2 red bell pepper (75g)
- 1 clove garlic (3g)
- 1/2 tsp sugar
- 1/2 tsp ground coriander
- 1/2 tsp ground ginger
- 1/2 tsp paprika
- 1/2 tsp vegetable oil
- 2 tbsp soy sauce (30ml)
- 2 tbsp balsamic vinegar (30ml)
- 2 pinches of sesame seeds
- 1 pinch of cumin seeds
- 1 pinch of black pepper
- 1 pinch of salt

Instructions:

1. Pour hot water over the glass noodles according to the package instructions. If you use lukewarm water, let them soak a bit longer until they are soft enough to your liking.

2. Clean and rinse the red onion, red bell pepper, and garlic. Slice the onion into half rings and the pepper into thin strips.

3. Thaw the shrimp and mussels, preferably in advance by moving them from the freezer to the fridge. Rinse them and remove any remaining shell or debris. Be sure to check the mussels for any sand or shell particles.

4. Prepare the garlic by either pressing it or finely chopping it.

5. Heat vegetable oil in a pan, then sauté the onion and red pepper for 2–3 minutes. Stir occasionally to avoid burning.

6. Add seafood and minced garlic to the pan. Mix well. After 2–3 minutes, proceed to the next step.

7. Pour soy sauce and balsamic vinegar into the pan with seafood and vegetables. Add ground

ginger, ground coriander, paprika, sugar, black pepper, and a pinch of salt. Mix everything and heat for 1 minute.

8. Add the drained glass noodles to the pan without excess water. Carefully combine everything to allow the sauce to soak the noodles. Remove from heat.

9. Serve the Asian seafood glass noodles hot, garnished with sesame seeds, cumin seeds, and freshly ground black pepper.

Nutritional Information (Per Serving): Calories: 380 | Fat: 9g | Protein: 16g | Carbohydrates: 56g | Sugars: 5g | Fiber: 5g | Sodium: 1260mg

Crab Patties

Prep: 15 minutes | Cook: 30 minutes | Serves: 4

Ingredients:

- 8.8 oz crab sticks (250g)
- 14.1 oz zucchini (400g)
- 2.1 oz semi-hard cheese (60g)
- 1 egg
- 1 tsp salt
- 1 tsp black pepper
- 4 sprigs of parsley (4g)
- 2 tbsp sesame seeds (18g)

Instructions:

1. Preheat the oven to 350°F (180°C).

2. Wash and dry the zucchini. Remove the stem and grate the zucchini coarsely. If using young and tender zucchini, there's no need to peel them. However, if the skin is tough, peel it off before grating. Add salt to the grated zucchini and let it sit for a while to release excess moisture.

3. Prepare the crab sticks. Slice them into small pieces.

4. Grate the semi-hard cheese using a coarse grater and add it to a mixing bowl with the crab sticks.

5. Wash the parsley, pat it dry with a paper towel, and finely chop it. Add the parsley to the mixing bowl.

6. Squeeze out excess moisture from the zucchini and add it to the mixing bowl as well.

7. Crack the egg into the bowl. Add black pepper. Mix the ingredients thoroughly. Note: No additional salt is necessary as crab sticks, cheese, and zucchini already contain salt.

8. Shape the mixture into patties using your hands and place them in an ovenproof dish. There's no need to grease the dish. Sprinkle sesame seeds on top of the crab patties.

9. Bake the crab patties in the preheated oven for 25–30 minutes or until they are golden brown on top.

10. Serve the crab patties with sour cream or Greek yogurt. For an additional sauce, try maconi (a type of yogurt-based sauce) with lime zest and fresh mint.

Nutritional Information (Per Serving): Calories: 380 | Fat: 12g | Protein: 15g | Carbohydrates: 40g | Sugars: 5g | Fiber: 4g | Sodium: 1200mg

Stuffed Tomatoes with Seafood

Prep: 15 minutes | Cook: 7 minutes | Chill: 1-2 hours | Serves: 4

Ingredients:

- 4–5 tomatoes (720-900g)
- 7.1 oz seafood cocktail (200g)
- 1 lemon (58g)
- 1 oz soy sauce (25ml)
- 0.5 oz olive oil (15ml)
- 1 green apple (182g)
- Bell pepper, to taste (150g)
- Salt, to taste

Instructions:

1. Boil the seafood cocktail. Place frozen seafood in boiling water. Wait for the water to boil again and cook for 7 minutes. Then, remove from heat and drain.

2. While the seafood cooks, wash the tomatoes, cut off the tops, and carefully scoop out the insides with a spoon. Cover the top opening with the cut-off piece, wrap in plastic wrap, and refrigerate.

3. Mix lemon juice with olive oil and soy sauce.

4. For the filling, dice the peeled apple into small cubes and mix with the cooked seafood in a bowl.

5. Add the dressing to the seafood and apple mixture. Mix well.

6. Cover with plastic wrap and marinate in the refrigerator.

7. Stuff the tomatoes with the seafood mixture. It's best to do this 1–2 hours before serving.

8. Serve garnished with lettuce leaves, lemon slices, and cherry tomatoes.

Nutritional Information (Per Serving): Calories: 380 | Fat: 12g | Protein: 13g | Carbohydrates: 56g | Sugars: 33g | Fiber: 11g | Sodium: 990mg

Stuffed Squid

Prep: 25 minutes | Cook: 20 minutes | Serves: 4

Ingredients:

- 2.2 lb squid (1 kg) s
- 2 onions (300g)
- 800 ml canned tomatoes in own juice
- 1 red bell pepper (150g)
- 5.3 oz smoked sausages (150g)
- 4 garlic cloves (12g)
- Olive oil (60ml)
- Salt, to taste
- Black pepper, to taste
- Parsley, to taste (60g)
- Smoked paprika, a pinch
- 2/3 cup rice (150g)

Instructions:

1. Thaw and clean the squid. If using fresh baby squid, separate the tentacles, chop them, and add to the filling.

2. Finely chop one onion and two cloves of garlic. In a deep skillet, heat two tablespoons of olive oil and sauté the chopped vegetables. Add thinly sliced red bell pepper and cook for five minutes.

3. Pour in the canned tomatoes with juice, bring to a boil, and simmer on low heat for twenty minutes. Season with salt and pepper to taste.

4. Prepare the filling. Clean and finely chop one more onion, two cloves of garlic, and the smoked sausages. If available, use Spanish chorizo sausages, but any thin smoked sausages will work.

5. In another skillet, heat the remaining two tablespoons of olive oil and sauté the vegetables with sausages over medium heat until golden brown. Remove from heat.

6. Cook any long-grain rice (such as Jasmine) until tender.

7. Add the cooked rice to the skillet with vegetables and sausages. Season with salt, pepper, and a pinch of smoked paprika for a smoky aroma and flavor. Mix well.

8. Stuff the squid with the rice mixture, packing it tightly, and secure with toothpicks.

9. In a deep and wide baking dish, pour the tomato-pepper sauce and place the stuffed squid on top. I used two medium-sized baking dishes.

10. Bake the stuffed squid in a preheated oven at 180°C (350°F) for twenty minutes.

11. Serve the stuffed squid hot, garnished with chopped parsley.

Nutritional Information (Per Serving): Calories: 380 | Fat: 12g | Protein: 29g | Carbohydrates: 40g | Sugars: 5g | Fiber: 4g | Sodium: 860mg

Braised Squid with Vegetables

Prep: 20 minutes | Cook: 20 minutes | Serves: 4

Ingredients:

- 1 lb squid, cleaned and sliced (450g)
- 2 tbsp olive oil (30ml)
- 1 onion, finely chopped (150g)
- 2 cloves of garlic, minced (6g)
- 1 red bell pepper, sliced (150g)
- 1 yellow bell pepper, sliced (150g)
- 2 medium zucchinis, sliced (400g)
- 1/2 cup white wine (120ml)
- 14.1 oz canned diced tomatoes (400g)
- 1 tsp smoked paprika
- Salt and pepper to taste
- Chopped parsley for garnish (10g)

Instructions:

1. In a large skillet, heat olive oil over medium heat. Add the squid and cook for about 2 minutes. Remove squid and set aside.

2. In the same skillet, add onion, garlic, red and yellow bell peppers, and zucchini. Cook until vegetables are soft, about 5–7 minutes.

3. Add white wine, diced tomatoes, smoked paprika, salt, and pepper. Stir well.

4. Return the squid to the skillet. Cover and simmer for 20 minutes over low heat.

5. Garnish with chopped parsley and serve.

Nutritional Information (Per Serving): Calories: 380 | 380 | Fat: 12g | Protein: 21g | Carbohydrates: 49g | Sugars: 10g | Fiber: 10g | Sodium: 700mg

Creamy Braised Squid

Prep: 10 minutes | Cook: 20 minutes | Serves: 4

Ingredients:

- 1 lb cleaned squid tubes (450g)
- 2 tbsp vegetable oil (30ml)
- 1 medium onion, thinly sliced (150g)
- 1 carrot, julienned (61g)
- 1 red bell pepper, thinly sliced (150g)
- 2 cloves garlic, minced (6g)
- 1/4 cup soy sauce (60ml)
- 2 tbsp sugar substitute
- 1 tbsp rice vinegar (15ml)
- 1 tsp sesame oil (5ml)
- 1/2 tsp red pepper flakes (adjust to taste)
- Sesame seeds and sliced green onions for garnish

Instructions:

1. In a large skillet, heat olive oil over medium heat.

2. Add chopped onions and garlic and sauté until softened.

Add the diced tomatoes and cook for 2-3 minutes, allowing them to break down.

3. Stir in the squid rings/strips and cook for another 2 minutes.

4. Pour in the low-fat sour cream and chicken or vegetable broth. Sprinkle paprika, salt, and pepper. Stir well to combine.

5. Reduce the heat to low, cover, and simmer for about 15 minutes or until the squid is tender.

6. Garnish with chopped fresh parsley before serving.

7. Serve hot over cauliflower rice or whole-grain pasta for a balanced meal.

Nutritional Information (Per Serving): Calories: 380 | Fat: 15g | Protein: 17g | Carbohydrates: 25g | Sugars: 9g | Fiber: 8g | Sodium: 660mg

Baked Mussels in Creamy Garlic Sauce

Prep: 15 minutes | Cook: 15 minutes | Serves: 2

Ingredients:

- 1 lb cleaned squid tubes, sliced into rings or strips (450g)
- 1 tbsp olive oil (15ml)
- 1 onion, finely chopped (150g)
- 2 cloves garlic, minced (6g)
- 1 cup diced tomatoes (canned or fresh) (180g)
- 1/2 cup low-fat sour cream (120g)
- 1/2 cup chicken or vegetable broth (low-sodium) (120ml)
- 1 tsp paprika
- Salt and pepper to taste
- Chopped fresh parsley for garnish

Instructions:

1. Preheat the oven to 400°F (200°C).

2. In a sauté pan over medium-low heat, melt the butter and sauté the minced garlic until golden. Remove and discard the garlic.

3. Add the light cream to the pan and simmer until slightly reduced.

4. Stir in the soft cheese until the sauce thickens. Season with salt and black pepper to taste.

5. Place the thawed mussels into oven-safe ramekins or small baking dishes.

6. Pour the creamy garlic sauce over the mussels.

7. Top with mozzarella cheese.

8. Bake in the preheated oven for 7–10 minutes, or until a golden crust forms on top.

9. Serve immediately.

Nutritional Information (Per Serving): Calories: 380 | Fat: 12g | Protein: 21g | Carbohydrates: 49g | Sugars: 10g | Fiber: 3g | Sodium: 780mg

Mussels in Creamy Tomato Sauce

Prep: 10 minutes | Cook: 10 minutes | Serves: 2

Ingredients:

- 2/3 lb frozen mussels, thawed (300g)
- 1-2 tbsp vegetable oil (15-30ml)
- 2/3 cup light cream (150ml)
- Salt and black pepper
- 2 garlic cloves, minced (6g)
- 1 medium tomato (140g)
- 1 tsp dried basil or fresh basil, chopped (0.5g for dried, 2g for fresh)
- Grated hard cheese (like Parmesan), optional for garnish

Instructions:

1. Heat the vegetable oil in a skillet over medium heat. Add the thawed and rinsed mussels and sauté for 2–3 minutes, allowing any excess water to evaporate.
2. While mussels are cooking, grate the tomato, discarding the skin.
3. Add minced garlic, grated tomato, and basil to the skillet and continue sautéing for an additional minute.
4. Pour in the light cream, season with salt and black pepper, and stir well.
5. Let the mixture simmer for 2–3 minutes until the cream slightly thickens.
6. Taste and adjust seasonings if necessary.
7. Serve immediately, garnishing with grated hard cheese if desired.

Nutritional Information (Per Serving): Calories: 380 | Fat: 28g | Protein: 9g | Carbohydrates: 23g | Sugars: 4g | Fiber: 3g | Sodium: 510mg

Marinated Mussels

Prep: 15 minutes | Marinade: 2+ hours | Cook: 0 minutes | Serves: 2

Ingredients:

- 1/2 lb thawed mussels(200 g)
- 2 tbsp apple cider vinegar (30ml)
- 1/2 cup water (120ml)
- 3-4 black peppercorns
- 1/2 tsp salt
- 1 bay leaf
- 3 tbsp vegetable oil (45ml)
- 1 garlic clove, minced (3g)
- 1/2 tsp smoked paprika

Instructions:

1. Mix water, vinegar, salt, peppercorns, and bay leaf for marinade. Cool to room temperature.
2. Blanch mussels in boiling water for 2 minutes. Drain and mix with marinade for 2 hours or overnight.
3. Heat oil, add garlic and paprika until fragrant.
4. Drain mussels from marinade and combine with aromatic oil. Serve.

Nutritional Information (Per Serving): Calories: 380 | Fat: 27g | Protein: 9g | Carbohydrates: 9g | Sugars: 0g | Fiber: 0g | Sodium: 820mg

Marinated Mussels

Prep: 20 minutes | Cook: 15 minutes | Serves: 2

Ingredients:

- 1/2 lb frozen shrimp, thawed (200 g)
- 2 1/2 cups Napa (700 g)
- cabbage, chopped
- 1 tbsp apple cider vinegar (or another 8% acidity vinegar) (about 15ml)
- 3/4 cup mushrooms, sliced (300 g)
- 1 medium-sized red bell pepper, julienned (200 g)
- 1 medium carrot , julienned (170 g)
- 1 tsp grated ginger (2g)
- 1 tbsp brandy (about 15ml)
- 4 tbsp soy sauce (60ml)
- 5 tbsp vegetable oil (75ml)
- Sesame seeds, optional for garnish (amount varies as per preference)
- Chopped green onions, optional for garnish
- 1 chili pepper, minced

Instructions:

1. Prepare all ingredients: chop cabbage, julienne bell pepper and carrot, slice mushrooms, mince chili, and grate ginger.
2. In a large skillet or wok, heat 1 tbsp of oil. Sauté ginger and chili briefly.
3. Add another tbsp of oil, then stir-fry carrot and red pepper for a few minutes.
4. Move veggies to a bowl. Add another tbsp of oil and stir-fry mushrooms until golden. Add brandy, stir, and transfer mushrooms to the bowl.
5. In the same skillet, add 2 tbsp of oil and stir-fry half of the cabbage until wilted. Add the remaining

cabbage and continue stir-frying. Season with a splash of apple cider vinegar.

6. Add the shrimp, stir-fried veggies, and soy sauce to the skillet. Cook until shrimp turn pink.

7. Taste and adjust seasonings. If desired, garnish with sesame seeds and/or green onions.

8. Serve with rice, if desired.

Nutritional Information (Per Serving): Calories: 380 | Fat: 26g | Protein: 14g | Carbohydrates: 23g | Sugars: 11g | Fiber: 7g | Sodium: 1540mg

Grilled Shrimp with Tangy Marinade

Prep: 20 minutes | Cook: 8 minutes | Serves: 2

Ingredients:

- 12 large tiger shrimp, thawed (around 450-500g)
- 1 inch ginger root, grated (about 10g)
- 2-3 garlic cloves, minced (about 9-13.5g)
- 2 tbsp olive oil (about 30ml)
- 1 chili pepper, finely chopped
- Juice of 1 lime (or lemon) (about 45ml)
- Salt to taste

Instructions:

1. Start by thawing the shrimp properly, preferably in the refrigerator for 12-15 hours.

2. For the marinade, mix together the grated ginger, minced garlic, chili pepper, lime juice, and olive oil in a bowl.

3. Add shrimp to the marinade, ensuring they're fully coated. Marinate for 30 minutes to 3 hours in the refrigerator.

4. Preheat grill to medium-high heat.

5. Grill shrimp for about 3-4 minutes on each side or until they're opaque and have a slight char.

6. Serve immediately, drizzling with any leftover marinade if desired.

Optional serving suggestions:

1. Accompany the shrimp with a mixed green salad or arugula.

2. Consider serving with a side of grilled ciabatta or baguette and a chilled dry white wine such as Sauvignon Blanc, Chardonnay, Pinot Grigio, or Chablis.

3. You can also prepare a garlic aioli sauce or purchase a tangy, slightly spicy mango sauce for dipping.

Nutritional Information (Per Serving): Calories: 270 | Fat: 14g | Protein: 26g | Carbohydrates: 7g | Sugars: 1g | Fiber: 1g | Sodium: 226mg

Shrimp and Vegetable Soup

Prep: 20 minutes | Cook: 40 minutes | Serves: 5

Ingredients:

- 5 cups of water (1180ml)
- 1.1 lbs of fresh shrimp, peeled and deveined (500g)
- 1.76 lbs of red fish (like salmon or snapper), filleted (about 800g)
- 1 cup heavy cream (240ml)
- 1 medium carrot, diced (61g)
- 4 medium potatoes, cubed (about 800g total)
- 2-3 stalks of celery, diced (200-300g)
- 1/2 cup of leeks, finely sliced (50g)
- 1 can (8 oz) of corn, drained (225g)
- 2-3 garlic cloves, minced (9-13.5g)
- 1 chili pepper, finely chopped (optional) or ground black pepper to taste
- Salt to taste
- 1/2 tsp ground nutmeg
- 1-2 bay leaves
- 2 tbsp fresh dill, chopped (6g)

Instructions:

1. Start by saving the shrimp shells and heads. Lightly sauté them in a pan without oil for 5 minutes.

2. In a large pot, add 5 cups of water, the sautéed shrimp shells and heads, and the red fish. Bring to a boil and simmer for 15 minutes.

3. In another pan, sauté the diced carrot, celery, and leeks in a small amount of unsalted butter until slightly softened.

4. Strain the fish and shrimp stock into the pan with the sautéed vegetables, reserving the fish. Add the cubed potatoes and simmer for 10 minutes.

5. Flake the reserved fish and add it to the soup, followed by the shrimp. Simmer for 2–3 minutes.

6. Add the drained corn, minced garlic, bay leaves, chili or black pepper, nutmeg, and salt. Bring the

mixture to a boil and then simmer for an additional 2–3 minutes.

7. Stir in the fresh dill and heavy cream. Bring to a quick boil, then remove from heat and let it sit for 10 minutes.

Nutritional Information (Per Serving): Calories: 428 | Fat: 19g | Protein: 40g | Carbohydrates: 28g | Sugars: 4g | Fiber: 4g | Sodium: 328mg

Zucchini Spaghetti with Shrimp

Prep: 20 minutes | Cook: 15 minutes | Serves: 4

Ingredients:

- 2 medium zucchinis (about 500g total)
- 3 garlic cloves, minced (about 13.5g)
- 1 red chili pepper, finely chopped (adjust to taste) (about 15g)
- 10 cherry tomatoes, halved (about 150g)
- 2 tbsp olive oil (about 30ml)
- 8.8 oz cooked shrimp (about 250g)
- 1/4 cup dry white wine (about 60ml)
- 2 tbsp lemon juice (30ml)
- Dried basil, to taste
- Thyme, to taste
- Salt, to taste
- 1 carrot (about 61g)

Instructions:

1. Using a spiralizer or julienne peeler, turn zucchinis and carrot into "spaghetti" strands.

2. Clean shrimp by removing heads, shells, and the dark vein along the back.

3. Heat olive oil in a skillet over medium heat. Sauté garlic and chili for about 1 minute, ensuring they don't burn.

4. Add shrimp and cherry tomatoes to the skillet. Pour in white wine and lemon juice, and cook for 1-2 minutes. Remove shrimp and tomatoes from the skillet and set aside.

5. In the same skillet, add zucchini and carrot "spaghetti". Cook while stirring for about 2 minutes, seasoning with basil, thyme, and salt.

6. Return shrimp and tomatoes to the skillet, gently mixing them in. Serve immediately.

Nutritional Information (Per Serving): Calories: 176 | Fat: 7g | Protein: 16g | Carbohydrates: 13g | Sugars: 6g | Fiber: 3g | Sodium: 248mg

Pasta with Shrimp and Mussels in a Creamy Cheese Sauce

Prep: 20 minutes | Cook: 25 minutes | Serves: 4

Ingredients:

- 8 oz pasta (whole wheat for more fiber) (about 227g)
- 8 oz shrimp, peeled and deveined (about 227g)
- 8 oz mussels, cleaned and debearded (about 227g)
- 1 cup light cream (or a low-fat alternative) (240ml)
- 1/2 cup grated Parmesan cheese (50g)
- 2 garlic cloves, minced (6g)
- 2 tbsp olive oil (about 30ml)
- Salt and pepper, to taste
- Fresh parsley, chopped (for garnish)

Instructions:

1. Cook pasta according to package instructions, until al dente. Drain and set aside.

2. In a large skillet, heat olive oil over medium heat. Add garlic and sauté until fragrant.

3. Add shrimp to the skillet and cook until they begin to turn pink. Add mussels and cover the skillet, allowing them to steam open.

4. Pour in the light cream and bring to a gentle simmer. Stir in the grated Parmesan cheese until the sauce is smooth.

5. Season the sauce with salt and pepper to taste.

6. Add the cooked pasta to the skillet and toss to combine, ensuring the pasta is well-coated with the sauce.

7. Serve immediately, garnished with fresh parsley.

Nutritional Information (Per Serving): Calories: 460 | Fat: 20g | Protein: 28g | Carbohydrates: 38g | Sugars: 2g | Fiber: 2g | Sodium: 560mg

Shrimp and Salmon Soup with Bacon

Prep: 15 minutes | Cook: 1 hour 10 minutes | Serves: 4

Ingredients:

- 7 oz salmon fillet, diced (about 198g)
- 7 oz shrimp, peeled and deveined (diced if large) (about 198g)
- 3 slices of smoked bacon, thinly sliced (about 90g)
- 1 medium white onion, finely chopped (about 150g)
- 1 cup light cream (or a low-fat alternative) (about 240ml)
- 4 medium-sized potatoes, coarsely chopped (about 600g)
- Salt, to taste
- Fresh thyme, for garnish

Instructions:

1. In a pot, sauté the onion and smoked bacon slices over medium heat until lightly browned.
2. Add the coarsely chopped potatoes and 4 cups of water to the pot. Bring to a boil, then reduce heat to a simmer.
3. Let the soup simmer for about 40 minutes, allowing the potatoes to become tender.
4. Add the diced salmon and shrimp to the pot and continue simmering for 20 minutes.
5. Pour in the light cream and season with salt. Allow to simmer for another 5 minutes.
6. Serve hot, garnished with fresh thyme.

Nutritional Information (Per Serving): Calories: 390 | Fat: 19g | Protein: 23g | Carbohydrates: 32g | Sugars: 3g | Fiber: 4g | Sodium: 750mg

Creamy Salmon with Cheese

Prep: 15 minutes | Cook: 30 minutes | Serves: 4

Ingredients:

- 1 lb salmon fillet (454g)
- 1 tbsp unsalted butter (14g)
- 2 garlic cloves, minced (6g)
- 6 oz cherry tomatoes (170g)
- 2 oz fresh spinach (57g)
- 1/2 cup light cream (or a low-fat alternative) (120ml)
- 2 tbsp mascarpone (or another soft cheese) (30g)
- Salt, Black pepper to taste

Instructions:

1. Prepare all the ingredients. De-skin the salmon fillet.
2. Sear the salmon in a preheated, dry skillet over medium heat for 2 minutes on each side. Season with a pinch of salt. Transfer to a baking dish.
3. In the same skillet, melt the butter. Add the minced garlic and cherry tomatoes. Season with salt and pepper, and sauté for 3-4 minutes, stirring occasionally.
4. Pour the light cream into the skillet and add the spinach. Bring the mixture to a light simmer.
5. Pour the spinach and tomato cream sauce over the salmon in the baking dish. Dot the top with spoonfuls of mascarpone or soft cheese.
6. Bake in a preheated oven at 350°F (180°C) for 18 minutes.

Nutritional Information (Per Serving): Calories: 380 | Fat: 26g | Protein: 26g | Carbohydrates: 10g | Sugars: 4g | Fiber: 2g | Sodium: 150mg

Soy-Marinated Salmon with Cheese

Prep: 40 minutes | Cook: 20 minutes | Serves: 4

Ingredients:

- 1 lb salmon fillet (454g)
- 1.5 tbsp honey (32g)
- 1/2 sweet red bell pepper, sliced thinly (75g)
- 3 sprigs fresh parsley, finely chopped (3g)
- Lemon slices, optional for serving
- 1.5 tbsp olive oil (22ml)
- 1 cup cooked rice (190g)
- 5 tbsp soy sauce (75ml)
- 1 tbsp sesame seeds, toasted (9g)

Instructions:

1. In a mixing bowl, combine soy sauce, olive oil, and honey. Mix well until the honey dissolves. For an added twist, you may add a few drops of Worcestershire sauce.
2. Pat dry the salmon fillet(s) using a paper towel. Place in the marinade, ensuring the salmon is coated on all sides. Let it marinate for at least 30 minutes.

3. Finely chop the parsley leaves and slice the red bell pepper thinly. Set aside.

4. Preheat the oven to 425°F (220°C). Lightly grease a baking dish with olive oil. Transfer the salmon into the dish and arrange the red bell pepper slices around it. Bake for 15 minutes.

5. After 15 minutes, baste the salmon with a couple of tablespoons of the remaining marinade, then return to the oven for an additional 5 minutes.

6. While the salmon is baking, fluff the cooked rice and mix in the chopped parsley. Season with salt, if desired. For aesthetic presentation, you may use a mold or a cup to shape the rice before placing it on the serving plate.

7. Once baked, transfer the salmon and red pepper to the plate with the rice. Optionally, you can drizzle the salmon with a thicker soy sauce or glaze for extra flavor.

8. Garnish the salmon with toasted sesame seeds. If desired, serve with a slice of lemon on the side.

Nutritional Information (Per Serving): Calories: 405 | Fat: 17g | Protein: 31g | Carbohydrates: 32g | Sugars: 11g | Fiber: 1g | Sodium: 1035mg

Pike-Perch with Mushrooms in Cream

Prep: 20 minutes | Cook: 25 minutes | Serves: 4

Ingredients:

- 1.5 lbs pike-perch fish fillets (about 680g)
- 14 oz (3.5 cups) white mushrooms or button mushrooms, sliced (400g)
- 1 large onion, diced (150g)
- 2 tsp vegetable oil (10ml)
- Fresh herbs (e.g., parsley or dill) for garnish
- 4 oz hard cheese, grated (consider using a reduced-fat cheese for a healthier version) (about 113g)
- 2/3 cup heavy cream (20% fat) (about 160ml)
- Black pepper, Salt to taste

Instructions:

1. Rinse the pike-perch fillets and pat them dry with paper towels. Remove any skin or bones, ensuring it's bone-free.

2. In a skillet, heat the vegetable oil over medium heat. Add the diced onions, sautéing until translucent.

3. Add the sliced mushrooms to the onions, seasoning with salt. Cook under a lid for about 5 minutes until mushrooms are tender.

4. In a baking dish, lay out the pike-perch fillets. Season both sides with salt and pepper. You may also add other fish-appropriate seasonings, if desired.

5. Spread the sautéed onion and mushroom mixture over the fish fillets.

6. Pour the heavy cream over the top.

7. Sprinkle the grated cheese uniformly over the fish and mushroom mixture.

8. Preheat the oven to 375°F (190°C). Bake for approximately 10 minutes, keeping an eye on the dish to ensure the fish doesn't overcook or dry out.

9. Once done, remove from the oven and garnish with freshly chopped herbs before serving.

Nutritional Information (Per Serving): Calories: 456 | Fat: 24g | Protein: 50g | Carbohydrates: 9g | Sugars: 4g | Fiber: 2g | Sodium: 387mg

Scorpionfish with Tomatoes

Prep: 20 minutes | Cook: 20 minutes | Serves: 4

Ingredients:

- 8 scorpionfish (the weight vary significantly based on the size of the fish)
- 2 large tomatoes (360g)
- 1 garlic bulb (separate 2 cloves and leave the rest unpeeled) (a garlic bulb is approximately 50g, cloves approximately 3g each)
- 4 oz hard cheese, grated (consider using a reduced-fat cheese for a healthier version) (about 113g)
- 2/3 cup heavy cream (20% fat) (about 160ml)
- Black pepper to taste
- Fresh herbs (e.g., parsley or dill) for garnish
- 14 oz cherry tomatoes(400g)

Instructions:

1. Clean the scorpionfish by removing scales and innards. Wash and pat dry.

2. Halve the cherry tomatoes and slice the large tomatoes.

3. Peel two garlic cloves, mince, and leave the rest unpeeled.

4. In a bowl, combine the tomatoes, minced garlic, rosemary sprigs, olive oil, and unpeeled garlic. Season with salt and pepper.

5. In a baking dish, place the fish and surround with the tomato mixture.

6. Preheat the oven to 392°F (200°C) and bake for 20 minutes. Serve hot.

Nutritional Information (Per Serving): Calories: 272 | Fat: 12g | Protein: 29g | Carbohydrates: 11g | Sugars: 6g | Fiber: 3g | Sodium: 340mg

Asian-Style Pike-Perch with Sauce

Prep: 20 minutes | Cook: 20 minutes | Serves: 4

Ingredients:

- 4 small pike-perch fillets (400g for 4 small fillets)
- 2 tbsp cornstarch (20g)
- 1/4 cup soy sauce (60ml)
- 2 tsp light sesame oil (10ml)
- 1/2 tsp grated ginger (1g)
- 4 sprigs cilantro, chopped (4g)
- 2 green onions, sliced (30g)
- 2 tbsp vegetable oil (30ml)
- 1 garlic clove, minced (3g)

Instructions:

1. If using frozen pike-perch fillets, defrost them in the refrigerator. Slice each fillet into four equal pieces.

2. In a deep bowl, combine the fish pieces and cornstarch, ensuring each piece is coated well.

3. In a skillet over medium heat, heat the vegetable oil. Fry the fish pieces until they develop a golden crust on both sides.

4. In a separate bowl, mix together the soy sauce, sesame oil, grated ginger, minced garlic, and chopped cilantro.

5. Once the fish is well-seared, reduce the heat to low and pour the soy sauce mixture over the fish. Stir gently until the sauce thickens.

6. Remove the skillet from the heat. The fish is now ready to serve.

7. As a side dish, consider serving the fish over steamed rice. Garnish with sliced green onions. For an additional touch, sprinkle with sesame seeds if desired.

Nutritional Information (Per Serving): Calories: 225 | Fat: 10g | Protein: 28g | Carbohydrates: 6g | Sugars: 1g | Fiber: 1g | Sodium: 749mg

White Fish in Garlic Sour Cream Sauce

Prep: 15 minutes | Cook: 35 minutes | Serves: 4

Ingredients:

- 10.5 oz buttery fish steak (300g)
- 1 medium tomato, sliced (100g)
- 1 medium bell pepper, thinly sliced (100g)
- 10 green olives, pitted and sliced (1.75 oz or 50g)
- 0.7 oz fresh cilantro, chopped (20g)
- 1 tbsp olive oil (about 15ml)
- 0.5 tsp dried oregano
- A pinch of black pepper
- 2 pinches of salt

Instructions:

1. Preheat the oven to 350°F (180°C).

2. If using frozen fish fillets, ensure they're completely thawed. Rinse and pat dry with paper towels.

3. In a medium mixing bowl, combine the low-fat sour cream, egg yolks, minced garlic, seasonings, and salt. Whisk until all ingredients are well-incorporated.

4. Place the fish fillets in a baking dish. Pour the sour cream mixture over the fish, ensuring the fillets are evenly coated.

5. Bake in the preheated oven for 35–40 minutes or until the fish is flaky and fully cooked through, and the top has a golden hue.

6. Remove from the oven and let cool slightly before serving.

Nutritional Information (Per Serving): Calories: 281 | Fat: 18g | Protein: 23g | Carbohydrates: 7g | Sugars: 4g | Fiber: 2g | Sodium: 596mg

Buttery Fish Steak with Vegetables

Prep: 10 minutes | Cook: 15 minutes | Serves: 2

Ingredients:

- 1.32 lbs white fish fillets (such as cod, haddock, or pollock) (600g)
- 1 1/4 cups low-fat sour cream (300g)
- 2 egg yolks (40g)
- 2 garlic cloves, minced (6g)
- Seasonings to taste (black pepper, dried herbs, paprika)
- Salt to taste

Instructions:

1. Begin by rinsing the fish steak and patting it dry with paper towels.
2. In a skillet over medium heat, heat the olive oil. Place the fish steak on the skillet and sear until golden brown on one side.
3. Flip the fish steak to sear the other side. Season with one pinch of salt and some black pepper.
4. Add the sliced bell peppers, tomatoes, and olives to the skillet alongside the fish.
5. Let the vegetables sauté for a few minutes until they start to soften. Add the dried oregano and the second pinch of salt.
6. Continue cooking for a couple more minutes, stirring occasionally to prevent sticking.
7. Once the fish is fully cooked and the vegetables are tender yet slightly crispy, remove from heat.
8. Stir in the chopped cilantro.
9. Transfer the fish and vegetables to a plate and serve immediately.

Nutritional Information (Per Serving): Calories: 473 | Fat: 22g | Protein: 58g | Carbohydrates: 7g | Sugars: 4g | Fiber: 1g | Sodium: 588mg

Sea Bass with Braised Sauerkraut

Prep: 15 minutes | Cook: 35 minutes | Serves: 4

Ingredients:

- 1.3 lbs sea bass fillets (600g)
- 1.7 lbs sauerkraut, drained (800g)
- 1 medium onion, finely chopped (150g)
- 1 apple, cored and julienned (182g)
- 2/3 cup apple juice (150ml)
- 3.5 tbsp sour cream (low-fat option) (50g)
- 2 tbsp butter (28g)
- 1 tbsp vegetable oil (15ml)
- 8 juniper berries (or a pinch of caraway seeds or allspice as a substitute)
- 2 bay leaves
- A pinch of sugar
- Lemon juice, to taste (amount varies)
- Salt and black pepper, to taste

Instructions:

1. In a deep skillet with a thick bottom, melt the butter. Sauté the finely chopped onion until soft and translucent. Sprinkle with a pinch of sugar and allow it to melt.
2. Add the drained sauerkraut and cook on medium heat for about 10 minutes. Pour in the apple juice, add bay leaves, and juniper berries. Simmer with the lid on for another 15 minutes.
3. Incorporate the julienned apple and sour cream into the skillet, stirring well. Continue to simmer for an additional 10 minutes.
4. While the sauerkraut mixture is cooking, rinse the sea bass fillets, pat them dry, and slice them into smaller pieces.
5. Heat the vegetable oil in a non-stick pan and fry the sea bass pieces for approximately 3 minutes on each side, until golden and cooked through.
6. Season the sea bass with lemon juice, salt, and black pepper.
7. Serve the fried sea bass accompanied by the braised sauerkraut.

Nutritional Information (Per Serving): Calories: 462 | Fat: 22g | Protein: 43g | Carbohydrates: 25g | Sugars: 15g | Fiber: 9g | Sodium: 1354mg

Greek-Style Sea Bass

Prep: 15 minutes | Cook: 25 minutes | Serves: 4

Ingredients:

- 1.75 lbs sea bass fillets (800g)
- 7 oz tomatoes (200g)
- 5.3 oz feta cheese, crumbled (150g)
- 1/4 cup plain yogurt (50ml)
- 5 sprigs of rosemary
- 3 tbsp olive oil
- 2 tbsp bread crumbs
- 2 lemon wedges
- Salt and black pepper, to taste
- 2 garlic cloves, minced

Instructions:

1. Blanch the tomatoes: place them in boiling water for a minute, then immediately transfer to cold water. Peel off the skin, quarter them, and remove the pulp. Dice the tomatoes finely.
2. In a bowl, combine the minced garlic, diced tomatoes, half of the crumbled feta, yogurt, leaves from half of the rosemary sprigs, and 1 tablespoon of olive oil. Mix well.
3. Preheat the oven to 400°F (200°C). Season the sea bass fillets with salt, pepper, and a squeeze from the lemon wedges. Lay some rosemary sprigs on the bottom of a baking dish and place the seasoned fish on top.
4. Cover the sea bass with the tomato-feta mixture.
5. Sprinkle with bread crumbs, the remaining feta, and drizzle with the remaining olive oil.
6. Bake in the preheated oven for 20 minutes if using fillets, or 30 minutes if using whole fish, until the top is golden and the fish is cooked through.

Nutritional Information (Per Serving): Calories: 381 | Fat: 19g | Protein: 40g | Carbohydrates: 11g | Sugars: 5g | Fiber: 2g | Sodium: 539mg

Oven-Baked Trout Steaks

Prep: 15 minutes | Cook: 20 minutes | Serves: 3

Ingredients:

- 1.32 lbs boneless trout fillets (600g)
- 2 tbsp unsalted butter, room temperature
- 1 tsp Dijon mustard (or similar mild mustard)
- 2 garlic cloves, minced
- 2 tbsp lemon juice
- Salt and black pepper
- 3 sprigs of parsley, leaves only
- 1/4 cup onion (40g)

Instructions:

1. Peel the onion and quarter it. Combine the onion, minced garlic, room temperature butter, lemon juice, parsley leaves, and mustard in a blender. Pulse until you have a smooth, spreadable paste.
2. If your trout is in one large piece, divide it into three even portions, roughly 7 oz (200g) each. Check the fillets for any remaining bones and remove them using tweezers. Season each fillet with salt and pepper.
3. Spread the onion and mustard mixture evenly over the top side of each trout fillet.
4. Preheat your oven to 400°F (200°C). Place the trout fillets on a baking sheet or in an oven-safe dish. Bake in the preheated oven for 15 minutes. After baking, let the trout sit in the turned-off oven for an additional 5 minutes to finish cooking.
5. While the trout is cooking, grill some vegetables like zucchini or tomatoes as a side, using minimal oil. Grilled vegetables or steamed rice make great accompaniments for this dish. Once ready, plate the trout steaks, add your sides, and serve immediately.

Nutritional Information (Per Serving): Calories: 318 | Fat: 15g | Protein: 40g | Carbohydrates: 4g | Sugars: 1g | Fiber: 1g | Sodium: 194mg

Tuna Pasta with Vegetables and Olives

Prep: 15 minutes | Cook: 20 minutes | Serves: 4

Ingredients:

- 10.6 oz pasta (300g)
- 10.6 oz zucchini, thinly sliced (300g)
- 1.1 lbs tomatoes (500g)
- 1 tbsp lemon juice (15ml)
- 5 sun-dried tomatoes
- 10 black olives
- 2 tbsp pesto sauce (30g)
- Salt, to taste
- 1 medium onion, thinly sliced
- 5.3 oz canned tuna, with its juice (150g)
- Black pepper, to taste
- 6 tbsp olive oil (90ml)

Instructions:

1. In a skillet with a thick bottom, heat 2 tbsp of olive oil. Sauté the thinly sliced onion for about 30 seconds. Add zucchini slices and cook for 5–7 minutes, until they have a slight crunch and not mushy.

2. Blanch the tomatoes by immersing them in boiling water for 30 seconds, then peel off the skin. Slice the tomatoes into wedges and add them to the skillet with the zucchini and onion.

3. Introduce the canned tuna, with its juice, to the skillet with the vegetables.

4. In a blender, pulse together pesto, sun-dried tomatoes, lemon juice, and 3 tbsp olive oil. Season with salt and pepper as required.

5. Boil the pasta in 8.5 cups (2 liters) of salted water with 1 tbsp of olive oil, following the package's cooking time instructions. Once cooked, drain the pasta.

6. Add the cooked pasta to the skillet with vegetables and tuna. Stir in the blender mixture and black olives. Mix everything well.

7. Let the combined dish sit for about 15 minutes for the flavors to meld. Garnish with chopped parsley before serving.

Nutritional Information (Per Serving): Calories: 496 | Fat: 24g | Protein: 16g | Carbohydrates: 57g | Sugars: 9g | Fiber: 7g | Sodium: 376mg

Baked Dorada (Sea Bream)

Prep: 25 minutes | Cook: 15-17 minutes | Serves: 2

Ingredients:

- 14 oz Dorada fish, cleaned and descaled (400g)
- 1 tbsp olive oil
- 3 pinches of salt
- 1 pinch of black pepper
- 1 lemon, sliced with 1 tsp of juice reserved
- 1 sprig of rosemary
- 2 sprigs of thyme
- 2 garlic cloves, minced

Instructions:

1. Clean the Dorada by removing scales, guts, gills, fins, and tail. Rinse thoroughly under running water. Ensure the gall bladder isn't ruptured to avoid a bitter taste.

2. Lay a baking tray with foil, place a few lemon slices on it to prevent the fish from sticking during baking.

3. In a small bowl, combine 1 tsp of lemon juice, 1 tbsp of olive oil, minced garlic, finely chopped thyme, and rosemary leaves. Season with 2–3 pinches of salt and some black pepper. Mix until salt is dissolved.

4. Apply some of the marinade inside the fish's cavity. Drizzle the rest over the fish. Place a couple of thyme and rosemary sprigs inside the Dorada. Optionally, you can also insert a halved garlic clove inside. For enhanced flavor, let it marinate for 15–20 minutes or refrigerate up to 24 hours.

5. Preheat the oven to 355°F (180°C). Bake the Dorada for 15–17 minutes. The baking duration might vary depending on the fish's size. Ensure it's tender but not overcooked.

6. Serve the baked Dorada warm. Garnish with a slice of lemon, a sprinkle of freshly ground black pepper, and a pinch of salt.

Nutritional Information (Per Serving): Calories: 293 | Fat: 11g | Protein: 41g | Carbohydrates: 2g | Fiber: 1g | Sugars: 1g | Sodium: 251mg

New Year's Cod Skewers

Prep: 20 minutes | Cook: 7 minutes | Serves: 4

Ingredients:

- 1.1 lbs cod fillet (500g)
- 10.5 oz cherry tomatoes (300g)
- 0.5 lemon, sliced, with some juice reserved
- 1 tbsp Narsharab sauce (pomegranate sauce)
- 2 pinches of salt
- 2 pinches of mixed peppers
- 2 tbsp olive oil

Instructions:

1. Rinse the cod fillet and pat dry with a paper towel. Remove any small bones and slice the thicker part of the fillet into even-sized pieces.
2. Combine olive oil, salt, mixed peppers, and a little lemon juice in a bowl. Gently toss the cod pieces in the marinade, ensuring they are well-coated. Refrigerate for 10 minutes.
3. Rinse the cherry tomatoes and remove the stems.
Thread the marinated cod pieces and cherry tomatoes alternately onto wooden skewers.
5. Preheat a grill pan. Cook the cod skewers on medium heat for about 5-7 minutes, turning occasionally until the cod is opaque and slightly charred and the tomatoes are just blistered.
6. Instead of grilling, you can bake the skewers. Add a small amount of water to a baking dish, and place the skewers over it, ensuring they're suspended above the water. Bake in a preheated 355°F (180°C) oven for 10-12 minutes.
7. Serve the skewers hot, garnished with a lemon slice and a side of Narsharab sauce for dipping.

Storage Tips:

1. If making ahead, store cooked skewers in the refrigerator for up to 36 hours.
2. For longer storage, freeze the skewers in a container for up to 4 months. Thaw in the fridge and reheat in the oven or microwave before serving.

Nutritional Information (Per Serving): Calories: 193 | Fat: 6g | Protein: 28g | Carbohydrates: 7g | Fiber: 1g | Sugars: 3g | Sodium: 271mg

Cod Patties

Prep: 20 minutes | Cook: 16 minutes | Serves: 4

Ingredients:

- 1.54 lbs cod fillet (700g)
- 1 garlic clove, minced
- 1/4 cup milk (60ml)
- 3.5 oz whole grain bread, crusts removed (100g)
- 1 tsp salt
- 1 large egg
- 1/2 medium onion, roughly chopped
- 3 tbsp vegetable oil
- 1 tsp white pepper
- 5 sprigs fresh dill, finely chopped

Instructions:

1. If the cod isn't already filleted, remove skin and bones. You will only use the fillet for this recipe.
2. Tear the whole grain bread into small pieces and soak it in milk.
3. In a food processor, combine the onion and garlic. Blend until finely chopped. Add the cod fillets and pulse until a smooth mixture forms.
4. Transfer the cod mixture to a bowl. Add the soaked bread (squeeze out excess milk before adding), egg, salt, and white pepper. Mix well.
5. Stir in the finely chopped dill until evenly distributed.
6. Using your hands, shape the mixture into patties, placing them on a plate lightly dusted with flour.
7. In a large skillet, heat the vegetable oil over medium heat. Once hot, add the cod patties. Cook for about 4 minutes on each side or until they are golden brown and cooked through.
8. Remove from the pan and serve hot, garnished with a sprig of dill. These patties pair well with roasted vegetables or pasta.

Nutritional Information (Per Serving): Calories: 295 | Fat: 11g | Protein: 38g | Carbohydrates: 11g | Fiber: 2g | Sugars: 3g | Sodium: 665mg

Pangasius on a Vegetable Bed

Prep: 20 minutes | Cook: 35 minutes | Serves: 2

Ingredients:

- 10.6 oz pangasius fillets (300g)
- 1.8 oz frozen green peas (50g)
- 1.8 oz frozen corn kernels (50g)
- 7 oz onion, sliced into thick half-rings (200g)
- 4.6 oz carrot, thinly sliced into rounds (130g)
- Salt, Ground black pepper, to taste
- Fresh rosemary, to taste
- 2 tbsp vegetable oil (30ml)
- 4.6 oz tomato, sliced into semi-circles (130g)

Instructions:

1. Thaw the pangasius fillets in the refrigerator. Once thawed, rinse thoroughly and pat dry using paper towels. Season both sides with ground black pepper and salt. Set aside.
2. Peel, rinse, and dry the onion and carrot. Slice the onion into thick half-rings and the carrot into thin rounds. Slice the tomato into semi-circles.
3. Lay out a sheet of aluminum foil. Arrange the onion slices at the center, followed by most of the carrot rounds, half of the corn and peas, and some tomato slices. Season with salt and pepper.
4. Place the seasoned pangasius fillets over the bed of vegetables.
5. Add the remaining carrot slices, tomato, corn, peas, and fresh rosemary on top of the fish. Drizzle with vegetable oil.
6. Carefully fold the foil upwards to enclose the fish and vegetables, sealing the edges to prevent steam from escaping. Bake in a preheated oven at 350°F (180°C) for 30–40 minutes.
7. Once cooked, carefully open the foil, letting the steam escape. Let it cool slightly, then serve the pangasius on its flavorful vegetable bed.

Nutritional Information (Per Serving): Calories: 389 | Fat: 15g | Protein: 31g | Carbohydrates: 36g | Fiber: 7g | Sugars: 12g | Sodium: 122mg

Seabass in Pesto Sauce with Vegetables

Prep: 20 minutes | Cook: 30 minutes | Serves: 2

Ingredients:

- 2 fish seabass, about 2.2 lbs (1 kg)
- 4 tbsp pesto sauce (60ml)
- 3 sprigs fresh basil
- ½ orange, thinly sliced
- 1.5 tbsp pine nuts (22.5ml)
- Salt, to taste
- 1 medium-sized eggplant (aubergine), thinly sliced
- 1 bell pepper, any color, sliced
- 8 cherry tomatoes, halved
- 1 tbsp vegetable oil (15ml)

Instructions:

1. Clean the seabass by removing its head, scales, fins, and innards. Rinse thoroughly under running water and pat dry with paper towels.
2. Coat the seabass with three tablespoons (or more) of pesto sauce, both inside and out, and transfer to a baking dish. Season the inside and outside with salt, adjusting according to the saltiness of your pesto.
3. Insert a sprig of basil and a couple of thin orange slices inside each fish. Add half a tablespoon of pine nuts or any crushed nuts of your choice.
4. In a mixing bowl, combine the sliced eggplant, bell pepper, and cherry tomatoes. Mix with the remaining pesto sauce. If desired, add a tablespoon of vegetable oil and season with salt.
5. Spread the vegetables around the seabass in a single layer in the baking dish.
6. To ensure a juicy result, you can cover the baking dish with foil. Bake in a preheated oven at 350°F (180°C) for about 25 minutes. If the seabass isn't fully cooked, extend the cooking time by 5–10 minutes. For a golden-brown finish, remove the foil 5–10 minutes before the end of cooking.
7. Before serving, garnish the dish with fresh basil leaves and the remaining pine nuts.

Nutritional Information (Per Serving): Calories: 537 | Fat: 27g | Protein: 59g | Carbohydrates: 18g | Fiber: 7g | Sugars: 8g | Sodium: 478mg

Fish Tagine

Prep: 20 minutes | Cook: 30 minutes | Serves: 2

Ingredients:

- 1.65 lbs white fish fillet (750g)
- 2 thinly sliced red onions
- 2 thinly sliced garlic cloves
- 2 tbsp vegetable oil
- 2 red bell peppers, sliced into thin rings or strips
- Salt, to taste
- 8.8 oz cherry tomatoes (250g)
- 3/4 cup black olives (200 ml)
- 5 sprigs finely chopped parsley
- Optional herbs like basil, oregano, or savory, to taste

Instructions:

1. Heat the vegetable oil in a tagine or suitable pot. Add sliced onions and garlic. Cook until they soften.
2. Place most of the sliced bell peppers on the onions. This will form a vegetable cushion for the fish.
3. Slice the fish fillet into serving portions. Place them on top of the vegetables. Season with salt and your choice of spices. If you want to maintain the fish's light color, choose herbs that don't impart a strong hue.
4. Place the remaining bell peppers, black olives, and cherry tomatoes on top. You can use whole cherry tomatoes for a more aesthetic presentation. If you don't have cherry tomatoes, regular tomatoes cut into quarters or sixths will work.
5. Cover and cook over low heat for about 25 minutes. Check the fish and if it's not fully cooked, adjust the cooking time accordingly. The vegetables will release moisture, but keep an eye on the dish to avoid burning.
6. Once cooked, sprinkle the tagine with finely chopped parsley. Serve your fish tagine with a side of your choice or enjoy it standalone.

Nutritional Information (Per Serving): Calories: 464 | Fat: 16g | Protein: 67g | Carbohydrates: 16g | Fiber: 6g | Sugars: 8g | Sodium: 1,363mg

Salmon Poke Bowl

Prep: 15 minutes | Cook: 0 minutes | Serves: 1

Ingredients:

- 5.3 oz salmon (150g)
- 3.5 oz avocado (100g)
- 3.5 oz cucumber (100g)
- Pinch of salt
- 0.7 oz fresh herbs (20g)
- 1 oz nuts (28g)
- Juice of ½ lemon (approximately 15ml)

Instructions:

1. Slice the salmon into equal-sized cubes. Make sure to remove the skin and any bones, if present.
2. Wash and slice the cucumber into semi-circles or cubes. If the cucumber skin is tough, peel it off.
3. Cut the ripe avocado in half, remove the pit, and dice it.
4. Wash the fresh herbs and nuts thoroughly. This is crucial as nuts may have traces of dust or other unwanted residues. If possible, soak the nuts in water to remove any bitterness and break down phytic acid, which can interfere with mineral absorption.
5. In a deep bowl, layer the diced salmon, avocado, cucumber, and fresh herbs side by side without mixing them.
6. Top the poke bowl with nuts, lemon juice, and a pinch of salt if needed.
7. Serve your nutritious Salmon Poke Bowl immediately for maximum freshness. Garnish with a slice of lemon if desired. You can also sprinkle with sesame or flax seeds for added benefits.

Nutritional Information (Per Serving): Calories: 470 | Fat: 31g | Protein: 30g | Carbohydrates: 24g | Fiber: 12g | Sugars: 4g | Sodium: 249mg

CHAPTER 8: BONUSES AND USEFUL MATERIALS

30-Day Grocery Shopping Templates for Diabetes

To make your journey easier, we've prepared these 30-day grocery shopping templates tailored specifically for individuals managing diabetes. With these ingredients, you can prepare the specified meals for the specified days. Adjust quantities based on your specific dietary needs and preferences.

Ensure to choose fresh, unprocessed items and always check labels for added sugars and preservatives. Planning meals with these whole foods will support a balanced and nutritious diabetic-friendly diet.

Happy cooking and healthy eating!

Grocery Shopping List for 7-Day Meal Plan

Proteins:

Eggs (for various dishes)
Salmon Fillets (for Salmon with Pine Nuts, Grilled Salmon with Vegetables)
Chicken Breast (for Creamy Mushroom Soup with Poached Egg, Light Chicken Broth with Vegetables, Baked Chicken and Roasted Vegetable Salad)
Turkey (for Turkey Medallions with Creamy Buckwheat & Spicy Vegetables)
Shrimp (for Seafood Medley Delight)

Dairy and Dairy Alternatives:

Greek Yogurt (for Greek Yogurt with Honey and Granola, Greek Yogurt with Chia Seeds, Dried Apricots, and Almonds)
Cottage Cheese (for Vegetable Omelette with Whole Grain Avocado Toast)
Parmesan and Feta Cheese (for various dishes)
Unsweetened Almond Milk (optional for porridge and oatmeal)

Fruits:

Bananas (for Whole Grain Oatmeal with Bananas and Almonds)
Oranges (for Chia Pudding with Mango Purée and Orange)
Mango (for Chia Pudding)
Berries (raspberries, strawberries for various dishes)
Lemons (for seasoning)
Vegetables & Herbs:

Spinach (for Scrambled Eggs with Spinach, Cheese Pancakes with Spinach and Parmesan Sauce)
Mixed Vegetables (zucchini, bell peppers, eggplant for Grilled Salmon with Vegetables, Baked Fish with Quinoa and Vegetables)
Mushrooms (for Creamy Mushroom Soup)
Fresh herbs (parsley, basil, thyme for seasoning)
Garlic and onions (for various dishes)
Celery (for Salmon with Celery Risotto and Wild Rice)

Grains & Bakery:

Whole Grain Bread (for toast)
Whole Grain Flour or Oat Flour (for baking)
Quinoa (for Baked Fish with Quinoa and Vegetables)

Buckwheat (for Turkey Medallions with Creamy Buckwheat & Spicy Vegetables)

Nuts & Seeds:

Almonds (for Greek Yogurt with Chia Seeds, Dried Apricots, and Almonds, Whole Grain Oatmeal with Bananas and Almonds)
Chia Seeds (for Chia Pudding)
Walnuts (for various dishes)

Pantry Staples:

Olive Oil (for cooking)
Balsamic Vinegar (for dressings)
Low-Sodium Soy Sauce (for flavoring)
Spices (cinnamon, pepper, salt, etc.)
Sugar-Free Sweeteners (erythritol or stevia for desserts)
Almond Flour (for Keto Almond Flour Croissants)

Miscellaneous:

Unsweetened Cocoa Powder (for Cinnamon and Walnut Biscotti)
Dark Chocolate (sugar-free, for desserts)
Honey (minimal use, for Greek Yogurt with Honey and Granola)

Grocery Shopping List for 8-14 Day Meal Plan

Proteins

Ground meat (for Meatballs in Tomato Sauce)
Chicken breast (for Crispy Chicken Schnitzel, Chicken Breast Stuffed with Spinach and Feta, Tender Chicken with Anchovies)
Turkey (for Turkey Cutlet)
Shrimp (for Grilled Shrimp with Tangy Marinade, Shrimp Caesar Salad)
Trout (for Pan-Fried Trout with Almond-Wine Sauce)
Salmon (for Salmon Poke Bowl)

Dairy and Dairy Alternatives:

Ricotta Cheese (for Pear, Ricotta, and Almond Tart)
Cottage Cheese (for Cottage Cheese and Berry Strudel, Almond and Berry Cottage Cheese Bake)
Yogurt (for yogurt sauce)
Eggs (for various dishes)
Butter (for cooking and baking)
Almond Milk (optional for smoothies)

Fruits:

Pears (for Pear, Ricotta, and Almond Tart, Pear Cake with Honey and Almonds)
Bananas (for Banana Berry Smoothie, Chocolate Banana Bites)
Berries (for Whole Grain Pancakes with Berries, Banana Berry Smoothie)
Apples (for Whole Grain English Muffin with Peanut Butter and Sliced Apples)
Avocado (for Avocado Spinach Refresh Smoothie, Tuna Salad with Avocado and Crispy Chickpea Popcorn)

Vegetables & Herbs:

Spinach (for Chicken Breast Stuffed with Spinach and Feta, Mushroom and Bell Pepper Frittata)
Mixed Greens (for Grilled Chicken Salad)
Broccoli (for Zucchini and Broccoli Fritters)
Zucchini (for Zucchini and Broccoli Fritters)
Mushrooms (for Tender Chicken with Anchovies, Mushrooms, and Lemon-Nut Sauce)
Cabbage (for Baked Fish Tacos)
Fresh herbs (for various dishes)
Lemon (for seasoning)
Pumpkin (for Meat with Pumpkin in the Oven)

Grains & Bakery:

Whole Grain Bread or Flour (for pancakes, muffins, and toast)
Almond Flour (for cottage cheese bake, frittata)
Quinoa (for Pan-Fried Trout with Almond-Wine Sauce)

Nuts & Seeds:

Almonds (for Pear, Ricotta, and Almond Tart, Pear Cake with Honey and Almonds)
Walnuts (for Pear, Ricotta, and Almond Tart)
Peanut Butter (for Peanut Butter Cups)

Pantry Staples:

Coconut Flour (for Coconut Flour Muffins)
Olive Oil (for cooking and dressings)
Balsamic Vinegar (for salads)
Anchovies (for Tender Chicken with Anchovies)
Chickpeas (for Tuna Salad with Avocado and Crispy Chickpea Popcorn)
Sugar-Free Sweeteners (for desserts)

Seafood:

Canned Tuna (for Tuna Salad)
Various Seafood (for Seafood Medley Delight)

Grocery Shopping List for 15-21 Day Meal Plan

Proteins

Salmon (for Salmon with Pine Nuts, Grilled Salmon with Vegetables, Cucumber Rolls with Salmon)
Turkey (for Turkey Patties)
Shrimp (for Bean Medley Salad)
Sea Bass (for Sea Bass with Braised Sauerkraut, Greek-Style Sea Bass)
Eggs (for Avocado Toast, Quiche Lorraine, Cheesy Omelet, Warm Bowl with Brussels Sprouts)
Dairy and Dairy Alternatives:

Greek Yogurt (for Greek Yogurt Parfait, Turkey Patties)

Feta Cheese (for Avocado Toast with Scrambled Eggs and Feta)
Cottage Cheese (for Oat Baskets)
Butter (for Lemon Tart, Quiche Lorraine, and cooking)
Milk or Almond Milk (for porridge and smoothies)

Fruits:

Berries (for Whole Grain Waffles, Greek Yogurt Parfait, Banana Berry Smoothie)
Bananas (for Banana Berry Smoothie, Banana Chocolate Bites)
Mango (for Chia Pudding with Mango Purée, Pan-Seared Tuna with Mango-Avocado Salsa)
Lemons (for Lemon Tart)
Oranges (for Chia Pudding)

Vegetables & Herbs:

Assorted Vegetables (zucchini, tomatoes, onions, bell peppers for Lavash Rolls, Baked Fish with Quinoa and Vegetables)
Brussels Sprouts (for Warm Bowl)
Avocado (for Avocado Toast, Cucumber Rolls with Salmon, Pan-Seared Tuna)
Fresh herbs (for flavoring and garnish)
Sauerkraut (for Sea Bass with Braised Sauerkraut)

Grains & Bakery:

Whole Grain Bread or Flour (for waffles, toast)
Lavash Bread (for Lavash Rolls)
Quinoa (for Baked Fish with Quinoa and Vegetables)
Brown Rice or Wild Rice (for Rice with Julienne)
Oats (for Oat Baskets, Flaxseed Porridge)

Nuts & Seeds:

Pine Nuts (for Salmon with Pine Nuts)
Chia Seeds (for Chia Pudding)
Almonds (for Almond Cookies, Nut and Fruit Roll)

Pantry Staples:

Olive Oil (for cooking and dressings)
Coconut Flour (for Coconut Flour Brownies)
Sugar-Free Syrup (for waffles)
Flaxseeds (for Flaxseed Porridge)
Sunflower Seeds (for Zucchini Pancakes)

Legumes:

Black Beans (for Bean Medley Salad)
Lentils (for Warm Bowl with Brussels Sprouts)

Seafood:

Anchovies (optional for salads or dishes)

Proteins

Eggs (for Poached Eggs, Turkey Patties, Sunny-Side Up Eggs, Cheesy Omelet)
Trout (for Oven-Baked Trout Steaks)
Chicken Breast (for Spinach and Strawberry Salad with Grilled Chicken, Mushroom Chicken)
Turkey (for Whole Wheat Turkey-Avocado Wrap)
Cod (for New Year's Cod Skewers, Cod Patties)
Pangasius (for Pangasius on a Vegetable Bed)
Sea Bass (for Seabass in Pesto Sauce)

Dairy and Dairy Alternatives:

Gouda Cheese (for Flatbread)
Greek Yogurt (for Zucchini Pancakes, Turkey Patties, Smoothies)
Cottage Cheese (for Cottage Cheese Dessert)
Kefir (for Mixed Berry and Kefir Wellness Smoothie)
Whipped Cream (for Grape Jelly)

Fruits:

Avocado (for Poached Eggs with Vegetables, Avocado Spinach Refresh Smoothie, Whole Wheat Turkey-Avocado Wrap)
Mixed Berries (for Smoothies, Cottage Cheese Dessert)
Bananas (for Banana Berry Smoothie)
Pears (for Pear Cake)
Strawberries (for Spinach and Strawberry Salad)
Oranges (for Pear Cake)

Vegetables & Herbs:

Spinach (for Flatbread, Sunny-Side Up Eggs, Green Risotto)
Tomatoes (for Flatbread, Cheesy Omelet)
Zucchini (for Zucchini Pancakes, Mushroom Chicken)
Artichokes (for Pasta with Artichokes and Spinach)
Various Fresh Herbs (for seasoning, Pesto Sauce)
Green Onions (for Cheesy Omelet)
Mixed Vegetables (for Grilled Vegetable Bowl, Dorada, Sea Bass)

Grains & Bakery:

Whole Grain Bread or Flour (for Toast, Pancakes)
Pasta (for Pasta with Artichokes and Spinach, Tuna Pasta)
Black Rice (for Mushroom Chicken)
Quinoa (for Grilled Vegetable Bowl)
Flatbread (for Flatbread with Gouda Cheese)

Nuts & Seeds:

Almonds (for Pear Cake, Oat Cookies)
Sunflower Seeds (for Zucchini Pancakes)
Seeds (for Fruit and Nut Bars)

Pantry Staples:

Olive Oil (for cooking and pesto sauce)
Balsamic Vinegar (for dressings)
Soy Sauce (for flavoring)
Spices (salt, pepper, paprika, etc.)
Honey (minimal use, for Pear Cake)
Oats (for Oat Cookies)

Seafood:

Seafood Mix (for Green Risotto)